C O M P L E T E
HORSE CARE
— M A N U A L —

COMPLETE
HORSE CARE
MANUAL

COLIN VOGEL

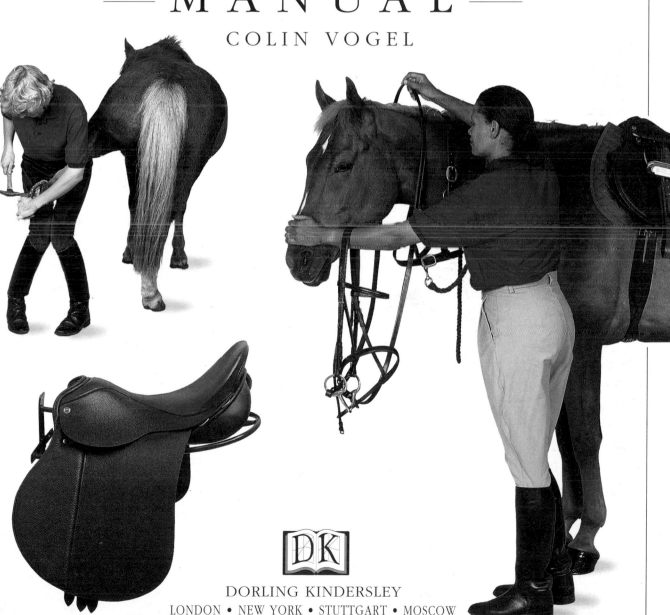

DORLING KINDERSLEY
LONDON • NEW YORK • STUTTGART • MOSCOW

The RSPCA and Horse Care

The Royal Society for the Prevention of Cruelty to Animals was founded in 1824. Education has always been an important part of the RSPCA's work, and a major focus is teaching people about the responsibilities involved in keeping an animal. Horse ownership is a huge undertaking, and prospective owners must make themselves aware of the responsibilities and commitment involved. This manual is a comprehensive and practical guide on all aspects of horsemastership, and is presented in clear, no-nonsense language. New and prospective horse owners can rest assured that the knowledge contained in this book will enable them to develop a greater understanding of what horse care is about.

Vince Cartledge, MA, BSc, VetMB, MRCVS
RSPCA Senior Scientific Officer

A DORLING KINDERSLEY BOOK

Project Editor Louise Pritchard
Project Art Editor Gurinder Purewall
Editor Katie John
Design Assistant Darren Hill
Production Hilary Stephens
Managing Art Editor Nigel Duffield
Senior Managing Editor Josephine Buchanan
Senior Managing Art Editor Lynne Brown
Editorial Consultant Gig Lees
Photography Andy Crawford and Kit Houghton

Photographed at Wellington Riding, Heckfield, Hampshire

First published in Great Britain in 1995
by Dorling Kindersley Limited,
9 Henrietta Street, London WC2E 8PS

Copyright © 1995 Dorling Kindersley Limited, London
Text copyright © 1995 Colin Vogel

A CIP catalogue record for this book is available
from the British Library

ISBN 0 7513 0213 9

Colour reproduced by Colourscan, Singapore
Printed and bound in Italy by
Arnoldo Mondadori Editore, Verona

CONTENTS

INTRODUCTION

THE DOMESTIC HORSE has always occupied an important place in human life. When horses were first domesticated, they probably had two roles. The slower, "cold-blooded" forest horses were beasts of burden. The faster, "warm-blooded" plains horses were a means of fast travel. Today, horses are no longer used in battle, the tractor has largely taken over in agriculture, and the diesel engine is the main means of transport, yet horses are still held in high esteem. Since horses were domesticated, people have bred them selectively to suit their needs or their concept of beauty. There are now several different types of horse and a large number of specific breeds that are recognized internationally. As in the past, different types of horse are better designed for different kinds of work.

Being in control of your horse

The relationship you build up with a horse must be based on respect, not on fear and pain, but until that relationship is established you must "con" the animal into thinking that you are in control. Once you show uncertainty, it will play up and test you. Your horse is probably bigger and certainly stronger than you. At 500 kg (79 stone) the average riding horse is six times heavier than an average man, so you cannot dominate one with strength. The horse must do what you ask because it wants to, or expects to, not because it is afraid of you.

Communicating with each other

A horse cannot be expected to understand exactly what you want it to do the first time it is asked. It will, however, know when it has done something right if you show that you are pleased. Try to understand what your horse is saying to you, too, by learning its body language. Communication should be a two-way process. Horses are not really intelligent; most are not problem solvers but they learn quickly. They have no concept of morality, so they learn what humans consider bad behaviour just as easily as good behaviour if they are allowed to. You must be careful not to allow a horse to learn that it can get what it wants through undesirable behaviour. For example, don't let it learn that if it threatens to bite you, you will let it have its own way.

Considering the horse's needs

When you agree to care for a horse you take on the responsibility of providing it with everything it needs. In order do this properly, you should understand how the horse lived in the wild. You will then be better able to provide an environment for the horse as near to nature as possible. You must know a little about the horse's structure and how the systems in its body work, learn to recognize signs of ill health, and know how to deal with injury or disease. You must also know how to use equipment and tack so that it does not hurt the horse. If the horse is happy in its home and in its work it will be more willing and able to do what you ask of it, and the two of you will enjoy a mutually beneficial relationship.

Chapter 1

LOOKING AT THE HORSE

Humans' appreciation of the horse's beauty of form and movement has inspired artists ever since the Stone Age. The picture opposite shows chariot horses on an Ancient Greek vase dating from the 5th century BC. At that time, artists did not know how a horse moved; a galloping horse was shown with its front and back legs extended together. Today, most people know this is impossible, but their knowledge of the horse's origins is still limited. A horse's anatomy, body systems, and natural behaviour are all adapted for a life as a wild herd animal and dictate how it should be cared for today.

DEVELOPMENT OF THE HORSE

The modern horse (*Equus caballus*) has been 60 million years in the making. That is how long it has taken its earliest ancestor, *Eohippus*, to evolve into the family *Equidae*. This family includes the zebra, the donkey, and the domestic horse, as well as the less well-known wild asses of Africa and Asia, and Przewalski's wild horse. It is thought that the immediate ancestors of the modern horse were three primitive types of horse. From these, two pony types and two horse types possibly developed; these, in turn, were the foundation of all modern types and breeds.

ANCIENT AND MODERN

Modern horse

Eohippus

Small ancestor
Eohippus was much smaller than the modern horse – only about 35 cm (14 in) at the shoulder. Instead of having one toe protected by a hoof, as a modern horse has, it had a pad with four toes on the forefeet and three on the hind feet.

THREE PRIMITIVE TYPES

Forest horse *(left)*
An important ancestor of some modern breeds was the Forest horse of northern Europe. It lived in woodland, where galloping speed was not important. It had large hooves to spread its weight on wet ground, and thick hair to protect it. It may have looked like this modern French Poitevin, which lives on marshes.

Przewalski's horse
Przewalski's horse is the only true survivor of the three early types of horse. In prehistoric times it lived on the steppes of central Asia and Europe. It has coarse features and a tufted tail – more like an ass than a modern horse. Small numbers have been bred in captivity since 1902, and selected groups are now being used to increase the wild herds.

Tarpan *(right)*
The Tarpan has influenced many breeds. We are probably indebted to it, via the Arab, for the refined look of our modern horse's head. The original Tarpan is extinct but attempts are being made to recreate it, as shown here. It evolved in semi-desert conditions in Europe and Asia and had a fine physique, necessary for travelling long distances in search of food.

DESCENDANTS OF FOUR BASIC TYPES

Exmoor pony
Height: 12.2–12.3 hh
(1.27–1.29 m)

Highland

Pony Type 2 lived in northern Europe and Asia. It was adapted to be resistant to cold and was heavily built. The Highland pony is thought to be a descendant.

Exmoor

The Exmoor, possibly Britain's oldest breed, is believed to be similar to Pony Type 1. This type lived in northwest Europe. It had a thick coat and bushy mane and tail to protect it against cold and wet.

Highland pony
Height: Up to
14.2 hh (1.47 m)

Akhal-Teke

Horse Type 3 was a tough horse that lived mainly in the deserts of central Asia. Its fine coat and slender build helped it to lose heat. The Akhal-Teke is probably a descendant.

Akhal-Teke
Height: 15.2 hh
(1.57 m)

Percheron

One of the largest breeds of modern horse, the Percheron is actually descended from the delicate Arab, which in turn is thought to derive mainly from Horse Type 4. This was a fine-boned desert horse that lived in western Asia.

Percheron
Height: 16.2 hh
(1.68 m)

TYPES OF HORSE

A breed is a distinct genetic entity. If one member of a breed mates with another, all their offspring will be similar in appearance to them. Humans have helped to fix horse breeds by mating selected animals and crossing their descendants to reinforce the horses' best features. Today, recognized members of a breed are entered in an official stud book. Horses that are not any specific breed may be described as a certain type. Types have a set of physical characteristics which happen to help them perform specific functions. Horses of the same type do not breed true when mated to each other, which means that their offspring will not necessarily have the same characteristics.

Riding pony

A miscellany of breeds can be mixed together to produce the riding pony. Most often the mixture contains Thoroughbred blood and native pony breeds. Some have more Thoroughbred in them than others, and are used primarily for showing rather than casual riding. By definition, a pony is under 14.2 hh (1.47 m); in competitions they are grouped in classes according to height, for example 12.2 hh (1.27 m) and under.

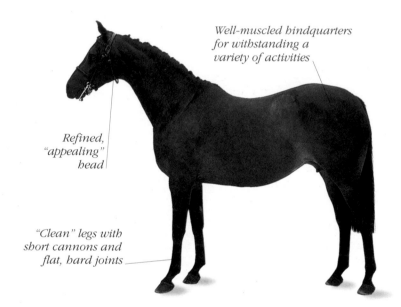

Well-muscled hindquarters for withstanding a variety of activities

Refined, "appealing" head

"Clean" legs with short cannons and flat, hard joints

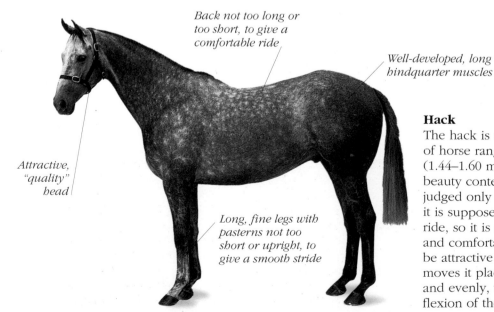

Back not too long or too short, to give a comfortable ride

Well-developed, long hindquarter muscles

Attractive, "quality" head

Long, fine legs with pasterns not too short or upright, to give a smooth stride

Hack

The hack is a light, elegant type of horse ranging from 14.1–15.3 hh (1.44–1.60 m). It is basically a beauty contestant, but it is not judged only on its conformation; it is supposed to be a pleasure to ride, so it is required to be obedient and comfortable. Its paces must be attractive to the eye. As it moves it places each foot precisely and evenly, with noticeable flexion of the knees and hocks.

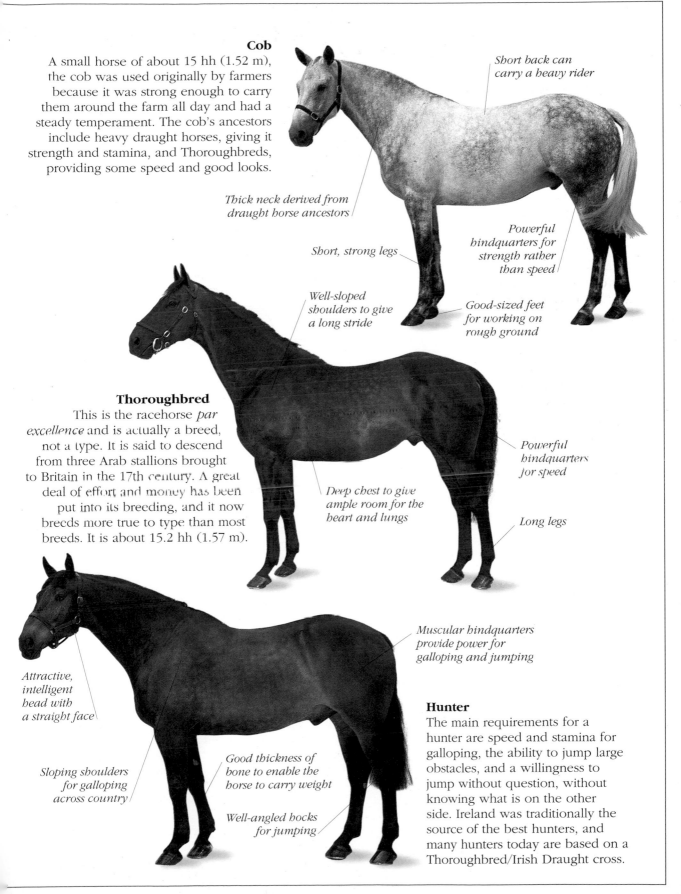

Cob

A small horse of about 15 hh (1.52 m), the cob was used originally by farmers because it was strong enough to carry them around the farm all day and had a steady temperament. The cob's ancestors include heavy draught horses, giving it strength and stamina, and Thoroughbreds, providing some speed and good looks.

Short back can carry a heavy rider

Thick neck derived from draught horse ancestors

Short, strong legs

Powerful hindquarters for strength rather than speed

Good-sized feet for working on rough ground

Thoroughbred

This is the racehorse *par excellence* and is actually a breed, not a type. It is said to descend from three Arab stallions brought to Britain in the 17th century. A great deal of effort and money has been put into its breeding, and it now breeds more true to type than most breeds. It is about 15.2 hh (1.57 m).

Well-sloped shoulders to give a long stride

Deep chest to give ample room for the heart and lungs

Powerful hindquarters for speed

Long legs

Muscular hindquarters provide power for galloping and jumping

Attractive, intelligent head with a straight face

Sloping shoulders for galloping across country

Good thickness of bone to enable the horse to carry weight

Well-angled hocks for jumping

Hunter

The main requirements for a hunter are speed and stamina for galloping, the ability to jump large obstacles, and a willingness to jump without question, without knowing what is on the other side. Ireland was traditionally the source of the best hunters, and many hunters today are based on a Thoroughbred/Irish Draught cross.

COLOURS AND MARKINGS

The coat of early horses was probably a certain colour to give camouflage in the wild and allow the horse to blend into its background and so hide from predators. A sandy-coloured coat still provides Przewalski's horse (see p. 10) with a good camouflage in its desert home. Most of the colours we see today have been developed by humans through selective breeding. Some colours are dominant to others; a foal will be the dominant colour if only one of its parents is that colour. Other colours are recessive; only if both parents are that colour is the foal likely to be too. The order of dominance of the main colours to each other is grey, bay, brown, then black. Chestnut is recessive.

BASIC COAT COLOURS

First impression

The colour of a horse is one of the first things used to describe it. Important factors in determining colour are not only the colour of the body, but also the colour of the skin, mane and tail, and extremities of the legs.

Bay
A bay has a black mane and tail and black lower legs, and is reddish brown over the rest of its body.

Dun
A dun varies from mouse coloured to sand coloured with a dark skin. It usually has a black mane, tail, and legs.

Chestnut
This is a reddish-brown horse with a similar-coloured mane and tail.

Brown
A horse with a black mane, tail, and legs, and a mixture of brown and black hairs over the rest of its body.

DORSAL STRIPE

A dark stripe along a horse's back is called a dorsal stripe, or list. Early horses had one, and the mark can be seen today on some dark-skinned horses.

Palomino
A golden-coloured horse with a much paler, sometimes almost white, mane and tail.

Blue roan
Roans have white hairs mixed with black (blue roan), bay (red roan), or chestnut (strawberry roan).

Dappled grey
Grey horses vary from white to dark grey and can be plain, dappled, or flea-bitten. All have black skin.

Spotted
A grey horse with black or brown spots, often called appaloosa. There is also a breed of that name.

Skewbald
The coat has large areas of brown and white. When the areas are black and white it is called piebald.

LEG MARKINGS

Extents of white

When describing the white markings on a horse's leg, it is best to refer to the top limit of the white. White areas are susceptible to infections because the skin, which has no pigment, is delicate.

White extending up to the fetlock joint – sometimes called a sock

White extending up the cannon – sometimes called a stocking

Markings on a white coronet – sometimes called ermine, especially if black

FACE MARKINGS

Official names

The only white markings on the face to have an official name are a star (any white marking between or above the eyes) and a stripe (any vertical white mark). A wide mark down the nose is often called a blaze, but for an official identification it is "a stripe the width of the frontal bones extending to both nostrils".

Star

"Snip"

Star and stripe

"Blaze"

"Freckled" stripe

HOOVES

Dark horn

Pale horn

Mixed horn

Horn variety

The hoof may have dark, pigmented horn, creamy, pale horn, or both. If both colours are present, the boundary is always a vertical one, with particular areas of the coronary band always producing the same colour horn. All horn is the same hardness.

EYES

Pigmented iris

Wall-eye

Pigment variety

The majority of horses have a brown-pigmented iris in both eyes. Irises with no pigment, or with a tinge of blue, are called wall-eyes. These can make a horse look a bit wild, but are no indication of character. The horse can see perfectly well.

PHYSICAL FEATURES

The relationship between the structure and function of a horse is referred to as its "conformation". The ideal conformation looks good and also works efficiently. In the wild, a horse must be able to move easily in its particular environment to find food and water, and escape quickly from danger for its survival. Humans can support and protect a domestic horse with boots and bandages, but it is more likely to perform well without strain or injury if it has a good conformation.

POINTS OF THE HORSE

Good conformation

A horse should have "clean", symmetrical limbs that can gallop at speed without the joints being jarred. A deep chest is necessary to contain the heart and lungs, and powerful hindquarters are needed for propulsion. Its head should be in proportion to the rest of its body, and its neck should be well set into powerful sloping shoulders.

Crest

Neck

Mane

Shoulder

Croup

Loins

Back

Withers

Dock

Point
of hip

Point of
buttock

Tail

Thigh

Sheath

Flank

Ribs

Elbow

Breast

Stifle

Gaskin

Point of
shoulder

Forearm

Point
of hock

Hock

Chestnut

Knee

Cannon

Tendons

Fetlock joint

Pastern

Wall
of boof

Ergot (small
protrusion at
the back of
the fetlock)

Coronet

Heel

SKELETON

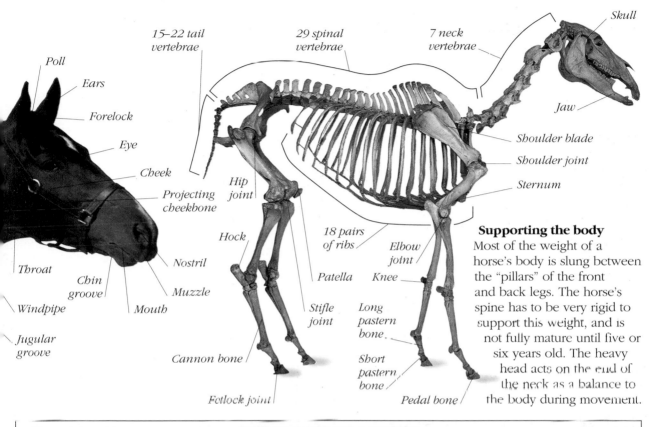

15–22 tail vertebrae

29 spinal vertebrae

7 neck vertebrae

Skull

Poll

Ears

Forelock

Eye

Cheek

Projecting cheekbone

Throat

Chin groove

Windpipe

Jugular groove

Nostril

Muzzle

Mouth

Hip joint

Hock

18 pairs of ribs

Patella

Stifle joint

Cannon bone

Fetlock joint

Jaw

Shoulder blade

Shoulder joint

Sternum

Elbow joint

Knee

Long pastern bone

Short pastern bone

Pedal bone

Supporting the body

Most of the weight of a horse's body is slung between the "pillars" of the front and back legs. The horse's spine has to be very rigid to support this weight, and is not fully mature until five or six years old. The heavy head acts on the end of the neck as a balance to the body during movement.

THE HEIGHT OF A HORSE

Hands and inches

Metres and centimetres

Measure at the highest point of the withers when the horse is standing square – ideally with no shoes on

It is useful to know a horse's height as part of its description and as a guide for the size of tack and clothing to buy. Horses are also grouped by height in showing and some jumping classes. Height can be given in hands and inches. Originally, a hand was the width of a man's hand, but it was standardized to 4 in (10 cm). Height is now also given in metres.

LEGS AND JOINTS

The main components of the leg are the bones, the muscles, the tendons, and the ligaments. In the horse's leg there are no muscles below the knee and hock, so long tendons link the muscles to the foot and lower leg to allow movement. The legs often undergo great stress; for example at certain moments when the horse is galloping its whole weight is taken by one leg (see p. 22), and severe tension is put on the tendons at the back of the cannon bone. Good conformation prevents abnormal strains from developing and causing injury.

STRUCTURE

Form and function
The upper part of the leg determines how it moves; the lower part how it bears weight. Joints allow the legs to bend and act as shock absorbers. Tendons link the muscles to the bones, allowing the muscles to move all the leg.

Muscle

Extensor tendon

Flexor tendons

Suspensory ligament

Hind legs

Flexor tendons

Suspensory ligament

Extensor tendons

Muscle

Forelegs

COMPARISONS

Legs to suit the horse
Although the leg joints of all horses have the same anatomy, they have adapted over the centuries to the role that their particular breed has to fulfil. As a general rule, thin legs are lighter for speed and are more easily moved. Large joints have a greater surface area over which to spread the weight of a heavy horse. Small joints on a large horse, or vice versa, result in problems.

Well-angled hock to absorb the impact of the foot hitting the ground

Fine joint for speed

Light horse (Arab)

Relatively upright hocks typical of modern draught horses

Speed is not important, so joints are coarse

Heavy horse (Ardennais)

Agility is important so the leg joints are fine

Despite the pony's small size, the knee is suitable for speed

Pony (Shetland)

GOOD CONFORMATION

The hind leg should be vertical at the cannon

The front leg takes more weight; it must be vertical to do so without strain

Forelegs

Hind legs

Important features

It is difficult to find a horse with legs that are perfect in all respects, but the better they are, the less likely they are to have problems. The horse should be able to stand four square, with the hind legs exactly behind the forelegs. Each pair of legs should match, with joints the same size and both legs truly vertical. Seen from the side, the legs should be straight, apart from the angle at the hock. The feet should not turn in or out, and there should be no swelling or puffiness around the joints and tendons.

BAD CONFORMATION

Forelegs

Conformational defects prevent the horse's weight from being evenly supported all the way down the leg. Instead, extra stress is put on certain areas. If a horse is over at the knee or back at the knee, its weight is shifted backwards on to the vulnerable heel region. Toes turned in or out put unequal strain on one side of the fetlock, pastern, and foot.

Over at the knee (too far forward)

Back at the knee (too far back)

Pigeon-toed (toes turned in)

Splay-footed (toes turned out)

Hind legs

If the hocks are too far under the horse, the muscles exert their maximum effort too early in the stride. If they are too far out behind, then the maximum effort comes too late to achieve proper propulsion. Cow hocks and bowed hocks weaken the propulsive force of the hind legs because the horse's legs want to bend more, rather than stay rigid.

Hocks too far under the body

Hocks too far behind the body

Cow hocks (turned in)

Bowed hocks (turned out)

FEET AND HOOVES

The horse's hoof is a variation on a claw or human fingernail. The rigid wall forms a broken circle, with the flexible heel region across the open arc. This allows the hoof to change shape slightly with the stresses of weight bearing. The horse's weight is actually suspended from the sloping hoof walls rather than supported by the soles. Although hind feet differ slightly in shape from front feet (they are more diamond shaped than round) they are otherwise identical in structure.

STRUCTURE

Side view

Front view

Coronary band

Wall

Toe

Heel

Bulb of heel

Bars provide support for the heel area

Seat of corn

Frog has a rubbery consistency and helps to minimize slipping

Cleft of frog

Sole is concave which helps the foot to grip the ground

Point of frog

White line is where the horn and sole join

The outer surface

The horn of the hoof is made up of a protein called keratin. It is formed by the cells of the coronary band in tubular structures that run vertically down the hoof wall. A healthy hoof has a smooth surface, without any horizontal ridges or vertical cracks.

The underside

The horn of the sole should be hard, not soft and flaky. The sole should be slightly concave, with the majority of it level with the wall of the trimmed feet. Contrary to popular belief, the frog does not play a role in blood circulation in the foot – it acts more as a spring, absorbing the percussion (shock of impact) as the foot hits the ground.

SIZE COMPARISONS

The size of a horse's feet can betray its breeding. The Arab/Thoroughbred lines have small, compact feet, whose walls should not be too upright or boxy. Heavy draught horses have large, broad feet, so that they sink into the ground less readily; the feet are often accompanied by feathers (long hairs down the pastern), even in crossbreds. Whatever a horse's build, the hoof wall around the toes should not be allowed to grow too long before it is trimmed. Overgrown feet will splay at the ends and sink at the heels, and this will result in abnormal stresses in the foot as a whole.

Foot of a light horse

Feathers

Foot of a heavy horse

Internal structure

The weight of the horse's body is transmitted down the straight column of bones that make up the pastern. That weight is suspended from the hoof wall by the laminae. The navicular bone and the deep flexor tendon that lies over it and holds it in place are particularly susceptible to abnormal stresses.

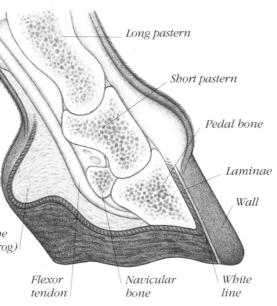

Long pastern

Short pastern

Pedal bone

Laminae

Wall

Plantar cushion (the internal part of the frog)

Flexor tendon

Navicular bone

White line

Close-up of laminae

The laminae link the pedal bone to the hoof wall. They consist of thousands of tiny interlocking leaves or fingers of bone and hoof, separated only by a thin network of blood vessels and nerves.

A BALANCED FOOT

Why symmetry is important

Every time a foot hits the ground, the impact sends shock waves up the leg. If the foot is not balanced, i.e. it is not shaped so that it sends the shock waves up the pastern parallel to the bones, abnormal stresses will be placed on the tendons, joints, and bones of the leg. Few horses have perfect feet, but proper care can prevent flaws from becoming problems.

Front view

Line A is an imaginary line down the front of the leg. It should divide the hoof equally. Line B, across the coronary band, should be parallel to line C, across the bottom of the hoof. This shape of foot means that shock waves are sent evenly up the middle of the leg, rather than to one side.

B   C

A

Slightly lop-sided foot   B   C

A

Correct proportions

Line D goes from the heel/wall junction to the centre of the toe, and line E goes across the widest part of the sole. These lines should be of equal length. If D is longer than E, the toe is too long; this puts extra pressure on the heel region.

E

D

Foot with a long toe

E

D is slightly longer than E

D

Side view

On the side view of a leg, an imaginary line F runs down the centre of the pastern. It should be parallel to line G, running up the front of the wall. If the lines converge or diverge, the horse is said to have a broken hoof/pastern axis.

F   G

F meets the ground about halfway along the sole

Converging lines indicate a long toe and collapsed heels, which means too much weight is on the heels

Broken hoof-pastern axis

F

G

GAITS AND MOVEMENT

The horse did not evolve for prolonged periods of movement. It spends most of its day grazing, and usually only when it needs to move to new pastures does it travel any distance. It is rare for a wild horse to walk or trot for more than five to 10 minutes without stopping. By trotting for 10 minutes a horse can cover quite a distance, certainly far enough for it to reach a new grazing area. Fear will stimulate a horse to gallop away from danger, but it cannot keep galloping for long, and it is not necessary for it to do so. After a few minutes it will either have escaped from the danger, such as a predator, or will have succumbed.

ARTIFICIAL GAITS

Just as humans have interfered with the look of horses, they have also developed artificial gaits. In most cases, these have to be taught to the horse. The paso, shown here, is a four-beat, lateral gait of the Peruvian Paso breed, which results in an exceptionally smooth ride.

WALKING

Four-beat gait
At the walk, the horse has three feet on the ground and only one in the air at any time. It places each foot on the ground in turn; first a hind leg, followed by the foreleg on the same side, then the other hind leg and finally the remaining foreleg.

TROTTING

Two-beat gait
At the trot, opposite fore- and hind feet hit the ground together in turn to give a two-beat gait. The fact that only one forefoot or hind foot is bearing weight at any one time makes this the best gait to use to detect lameness (see p. 120).

CANTERING

Three-beat gait
At the canter, two diagonal feet hit the ground together. The other two feet hit the ground separately, making a three-beat gait. One forefoot is followed by the opposite hind foot, then the other two feet together. There is a time when no feet are on the ground.

GALLOPING

Four-beat gait
This follows the same pattern as the canter, but the paired limbs do not hit the ground together. The hind limb lands slightly before the paired forelimb, making a four-beat gait. In the gallop and the canter, a horse can change the leading foreleg.

TEETH AND JAWS

The horse relies a great deal on its teeth. Its digestive juices cannot break down the cellulose in grass, so this is done by bacteria in its colon. If the teeth do not break down the herbage to a thick "soup", then the bacteria will not be able to work on it, the horse will get no goodness from it, and the fibrous material may become wedged in the intestines. The lack of good functional teeth is probably one of the major reasons why a horse may not live to an old age in the wild.

DIFFERENT TEETH

Function of the teeth

The horse's upper and lower jaw are basically a mirror image of each other in terms of teeth. Each has six incisor teeth (three on each side). These are the teeth that cut food. In the adult horse there are six premolar and six molar teeth (three of each on each side). These are the teeth that chew food. In the young horse, the back three molars are not present. In male horses, there may be one canine tooth on each side. These have no function.

Adult upper jaw from below

Molars (found only in adult horses)

Premolars (found in horses of all ages)

Wolf tooth (very small if present at all, and with only a short root)

Incisors (found in all horses)

Diastema (the space where the bit conveniently fits – also known as the bars of the mouth)

Area of sinuses

Canine tooth (not usually present in mares)

Teeth and the skull

In order to reduce the weight of its large skull, the horse has three air-filled sinuses on each side. These lie in front of the eyes. The roots of most of the molar teeth extend up into these sinuses.

Skull from the side

Upper canine

Upper incisors

Molars

Premolars

Lower canine

Lower incisors

THE INCISORS

Teeth meet at the front

Teeth do not meet properly which makes biting difficult

Teeth that meet

The incisor teeth must meet their counterpart in the opposite jaw if they are to cut properly. This is especially important for horses in the wild, because if they cannot cut grass they cannot get any food. Domestic horses can have food cut up for them.

Teeth that do not meet

In some horses, the upper jaw is longer than the lower jaw, causing the upper teeth to be in front of the lower teeth. A horse with this problem is called parrot-mouthed. When, more rarely, the lower jaw is longer, the horse is called sow-mouthed.

TEETH AS AN INDICATOR OF AGE

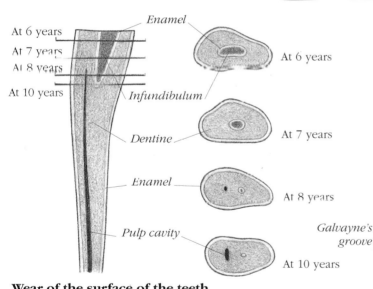

At 6 years
At 7 years
At 8 years
At 10 years

Enamel

Infundibulum

Dentine

Enamel

Pulp cavity

At 6 years

At 7 years

At 8 years

Galvayne's groove

At 10 years

Milk tooth

The straight teeth of a four-year-old horse

The angled teeth of a 20-year-old horse

Wear of the surface of the teeth

A horse's teeth can be used as a means of estimating its age, although the estimate can be only approximate. The cutting surface of the incisor teeth becomes worn down with age, revealing a different cross-section as it does so. This can help in ageing a horse up to the age of eight. From then on, the horse will be officially referred to as "aged". The older a horse is, the more angled its front teeth will be. At about the age of 10, a mark known as Galvayne's groove appears at the top of the upper corner incisors. It gradually grows to the bottom, then starts to disappear from the top.

Temporary and permanent teeth

A foal has a set of milk teeth, which are gradually replaced by permanent teeth – all of them usually by the age of five. A horse's bones are mature at the same age. The number of milk teeth present is therefore a guide to how much work a horse should do.

BODY SYSTEMS

As the horse evolved, its body systems adapted for its particular needs. For example, as a grazing animal, its digestive system had to be able to digest cellulose, so the large colon became a reservoir for bacterial fermentation. As a "fight or flight" animal, the horse's muscles sometimes needed extra oxygen suddenly, so the spleen developed to store red blood cells and push them into the blood on demand.

RESPIRATION AND CIRCULATION

Working together

The respiratory and circulatory functions are inextricably inter-related. There is no point in oxygen being extracted from the air breathed in, which is the role of the respiratory system, unless that oxygen can be delivered to the body cells, which is the role of the circulatory system. The underlying principle is that gases move from where they are in a high concentration to where they are in a low concentration. Oxygen from the air passes through the walls of the lungs into the blood, which is pumped around the body by the heart. At the same time, carbon dioxide passes from the blood into the lungs and is breathed out.

Windpipe

Oxygen-depleted blood

Oxygen-rich blood

Brain

Spinal cord

Lung capillaries

Heart

Oxygen-rich blood (red)

Capillaries in the body

Oxygen-depleted blood (blue)

Diagram of blood circulation

Heart

Lungs

Blood circulation

The heart is really two pumps. It has two ventricles supplying two circulatory systems. In one system, oxygen-depleted blood is circulated through the lungs, where it picks up oxygen and releases carbon dioxide. In the second system, oxygen-rich blood is circulated around the body releasing oxygen and collecting carbon dioxide.

NERVOUS SYSTEM

Instructing the body

The nervous system coordinates all the activities of the body. It receives information via the senses, decides what action is needed, and then sends instructions to the relevant system to achieve that end. Most of the nervous system's work is automatic.

Cerebellum controls muscle activity and balance

Brain stem controls automatic tasks such as breathing

The brain

Cerebrum does the thinking

DIGESTIVE SYSTEM

The process of digestion

The horse needs only a small stomach because food passes quickly to the small intestine for digestion. Undigested fibre passes to the caecum and the large colon to be broken down. Fluid is absorbed into the blood and the dry remains are expelled as dung.

Products of digestion are absorbed into the blood from the caecum

The caecum

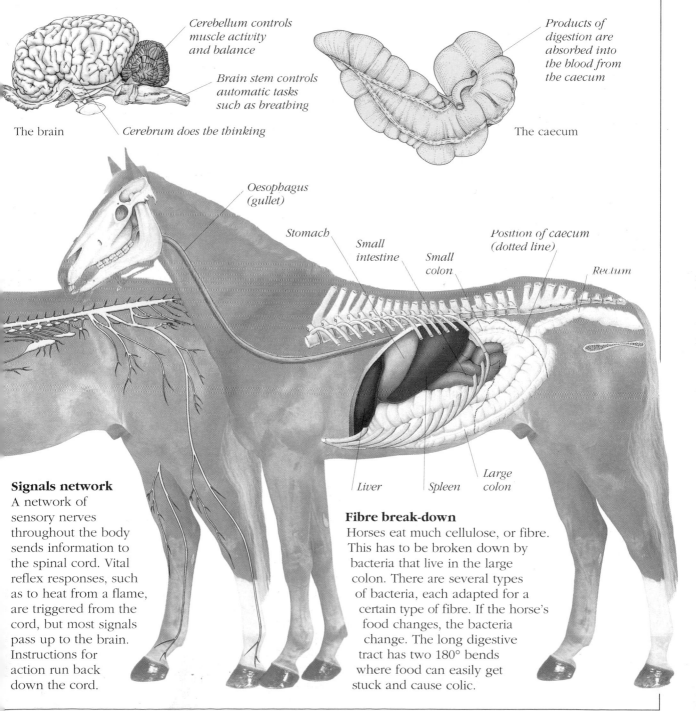

Oesophagus (gullet)

Stomach

Small intestine

Small colon

Position of caecum (dotted line)

Rectum

Liver

Spleen

Large colon

Signals network

A network of sensory nerves throughout the body sends information to the spinal cord. Vital reflex responses, such as to heat from a flame, are triggered from the cord, but most signals pass up to the brain. Instructions for action run back down the cord.

Fibre break-down

Horses eat much cellulose, or fibre. This has to be broken down by bacteria that live in the large colon. There are several types of bacteria, each adapted for a certain type of fibre. If the horse's food changes, the bacteria change. The long digestive tract has two 180° bends where food can easily get stuck and cause colic.

THE HEALTHY HORSE

A healthy horse is one whose natural physical capabilities are not restricted by accident or disease. In the wild, there is a sharp distinction between healthy and unhealthy horses. The healthy ones survive and the unhealthy ones succumb to predators and diseases. Among domestic horses, this distinction is much more blurred; even very ill horses may survive, thanks to veterinary care. Do not confuse health with fitness; a healthy horse is not necessarily a fit one. A fit horse's performance is not restricted by fatigue, while there are many healthy horses that are easily tired by exercise. A healthy horse should be neither too fat nor too thin (see p. 109). Particularly the former can lead to health problems in horses, just as it does in humans. Old horses tend to be more susceptible to disease, so you must watch them carefully to spot even the slightest variation from their normal healthy appearance or behaviour. Beware of putting any potential symptom down to "just old age".

Temperature, pulse rate, and respiration rate
These are important signs of health or illness. Learn what your horse's rates are by measuring them when you know the horse is healthy (see p. 43). The normal rates in a healthy horse at rest are: Temperature: 38.3–38.6°C (101–101.5°F); Pulse rate: 30–50 beats per minute; Respiratory rate: 8–16 breaths per minute.

Tail
The tail should be shiny, and active in removing any flies. It should not be clamped down between the legs or stained and matted with loose faeces. When the horse trots away, the tail should not be held to one side or the other, which could indicate pain somewhere. Watch out for rubbed or bare patches on the dock; these could be a sign of worms or sweet itch (see p. 131).

Droppings and urine
A healthy horse's droppings form balls which break as they hit the ground. They contain no fibrous lumps or whole cereal grains and are produced 6–10 times every 24 hours. Urine smells strongly and is dark yellow and cloudy.

Ears

A horse's ears should be alert and follow you around, just like another pair of eyes. The sense of hearing is just as valuable to a horse as its sight.

Eyes

The eyes should be bright, with no discharge. It is normal for there to be cauliflower-shaped black bodies hanging from the top of the iris. These are called the *corpora nigra*. The membrane around the eye and inside the eyelid should be salmon-pink.

Mouth and nostrils

Most horses have fixed eating habits, and they do not change their behaviour unless something is wrong. They should not drop food out of their mouth while eating – a problem known as quidding (see p. 129). The nostrils should not be flared whilst the horse is at rest, and there should be no discharge.

Skin and coat

The skin should be supple and move easily. If you pick up a fold of skin over the neck and release it, the fold should immediately flatten out again. (If it stays raised the horse is probably dehydrated.) The coat should be smooth and shiny rather than "staring" (dull), with no loose hair unless the horse is moulting.

Feet

Healthy horses are happy to take weight on all four feet, although they take 60 per cent of their weight on their front feet. Many horses habitually rest a hind foot more than the others. The hooves should not have any horizontal grooves or vertical cracks, and the horn must not be broken or split where it meets the ground.

EQUINE SENSES

Horses in the wild rely on their senses – sight, hearing, touch, smell, and taste – for survival. Sight and sound warn of danger, and taste and smell identify safe or bad food. Domestication has dulled their response to some of these, for example they may not run away every time they see a car, but their senses are just as acute as ever. When a horse reacts to something that we haven't noticed, it is often put down to its "sixth sense". It is really the horse's extremely sharp senses working together to process bits of information that we have missed.

SIGHT

Bifocal vision

Range of vision of left eye

Range of vision of right eye

Field of vision
A horse's eyes work independently of each other. Each covers a wide field of vision over a full semi-circle. There is a small overlap in front of the face, and a "blind spot" directly behind. Never approach a horse from behind, because you will startle it.

Seeing straight ahead
A horse makes little use of stereoscopic vision for judging distances, for example when jumping, so a one-eyed horse can still judge distances. A horse loses sight of a fence as it takes off, so it has to trust in its rider knowing it is safe to jump.

HEARING

The mobile ears, wide range of vision, and flexible neck allow the horse to keep informed of what is happening behind it

Use of the ears
Horses use their sense of hearing a great deal, moving each ear independently to pick up sound waves. Talking to a horse is a good way to let it know that you are there and that you are not a threat.

Preparing to flee
When a horse hears a sound, such as a dog barking, it lifts its head, looks towards the source, and assesses the significance of the noise. It will not turn its whole body because it would then be less able to run away from the danger.

TOUCH

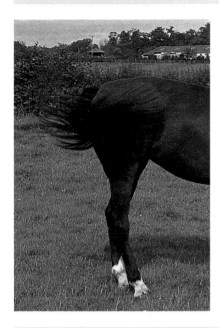

Sensitivity
The horse has an acute sense of touch over its whole body. It can detect the presence of a single fly and whisk it away with its tail with unerring accuracy. You should not be surprised, therefore, if your horse is startled if you touch it with no warning.

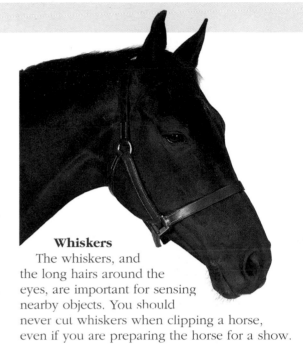

Whiskers
The whiskers, and the long hairs around the eyes, are important for sensing nearby objects. You should never cut whiskers when clipping a horse, even if you are preparing the horse for a show.

SMELL

Obtaining information
Smell enables a horse to detect undesirable items in its food. It is also important in social interactions; horses greet friends or identify strangers by touching muzzle to muzzle.

Scent analysis
This action, known as flehmen, may involve "smelling" with the sensitive membranes inside the lips, as well as the nostrils. It is usually seen in sexual activity, so it may detect pheromones, the sex hormones released into the air. Many horses will do this when they come across an unusual smell or feed for the first time.

TASTE

Favourite foods
Horses like salty and sweet things but not bitter or sour ones. Many horses like peppermints. This may be because they once licked someone's hand, which was salty, received a peppermint as a bonus, and came to associate the taste with nice people.

BODY LANGUAGE

The horse is a herd animal, and needs to be able to communicate with other herd members. Of course horses do not have philosophical discussions – they need only to convey basic emotions, such as fear, and establish a hierarchy of dominance without resorting to violence. Domestic horses treat us as members of their herd, so use the same body language to us.

CONTENTMENT

Signs of happiness
A contented horse is not worried about any other horses that may be around. It shows off its best features by carrying its head high and holding its tail up, and tends to make its movements more extravagant than usual.

In the field
Because horses like company, they are usually pleased when they see a human being whom they recognize and trust. They will approach you without fear, rather than running away from you.

In the stable
If a horse wants to be left alone to enjoy a rest, it will turn away from other horses. A stabled horse may turn its back to the door to show you that it does not want to talk.

IMPATIENCE

A nudge can be a powerful push

Head movements
Like children, horses may not like being ignored. A horse may demand a human's attention by nudging with its muzzle.

Stamping feet
A horse can get impatient waiting for food or when restricted. It may then stamp or kick the stable door to make a noise.

ANNOYANCE

Ears back

Teeth bared

Biting other horses

When its patience is exhausted, a horse may express anger by biting. The horse's teeth are not designed to cause wounds when it does this, as a carnivore's might, but the bite says, "I have a position within the herd that allows me to bite you if I want to."

Biting you

A horse may bite you for the same reason as it would bite a horse. Never tolerate this – it would tell the horse that you accept it as boss. Distract it before it bites; if it does get you, slap its muzzle.

FRIGHT OR FURY?

White of eye visible

Body ready for action

Signs of fright and aggression

There is a big difference between an aggressive and a frightened horse, although both may show the white of their eye and bite or kick. A scared horse will stand its ground or run away. It is very unusual for a horse to be aggressive, but if one is, it will move towards you. A frightened horse is more likely to run away: wait for it to come to you, no matter how long it takes.

UNHAPPINESS

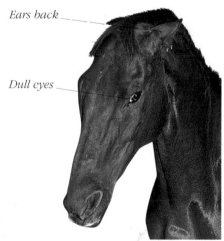

Ears back

Dull eyes

Causes of unhappiness

Horses can get depressed during illness or if bullied. They will look uninterested and unhappy, and may become aggressive. Riders used to boast about breaking a horse's spirit, but this is just not acceptable today.

THE HORSE AT LEISURE

Even with the finest stable management, horses need periods of rest from their work for humans. This may involve letting them out in a field for an hour every afternoon, or turning them out for days or weeks. You should never suddenly change a horse's routine from strenuous and regular work to field rest; you must allow its digestive and movement systems to adapt over at least a week. Most horses thrive at grass (except for a few Thoroughbred-type horses which cannot adapt, just as workaholic people cannot relax on holiday). Many horses perform at their best when they return after a rest period. Whether this is due to mental relaxation in a more natural state, or because the access to grazing provides good natural nutrition, is not known. We often give "Dr Green" the credit anyway.

RELAXING

Sunbathing
Horses at grass lie down much more often than stabled horses, especially in sunny weather. When relaxing in this way they may look unconscious, but if you make a sudden noise, you will see that they are awake enough to be aware of possible danger.

Playing
Young horses learn their communication skills from play. Like all youngsters they have mock fights. They also seek a lot of physical contact. This is a point to remember if keeping a solitary horse; because it has no horse friends, its owner must provide all social contact.

ROLLING

Why do horses roll?
Horses roll for pleasure. They also roll when they have colic, or abdominal pain. If you regularly watch a horse both before and after it rolls, you should have very little trouble telling which kind of roll it is. Rolling involves almost all the muscles of the body, and when horses roll for pleasure they seem to enoy it in the same way as humans would enjoy a good stretch. Horses also roll to rub their back, and often roll in dust for a cleansing bath.

Choosing the place
A horse often uses one particular spot every time. Like a dog settling on its bed, it may turn around on the spot once or twice.

Settling down
A horse goes down front first. It may be that this leaves its hind legs ready to operate in case it suddenly has to run from danger.

STABLE VICES

Horses that have little stimulation get bored and some develop vices as a result. These are repetitive behaviour patterns or movements such as weaving (swinging the head from side to side) and wind-sucking (gulping in air). Some horses fix their jaws on a solid object, such as a post, and arch their neck, often wind-sucking too. This is called crib-biting. Most vices start in the stable, but may also be shown in the field.

Crib-biting

The ears are laid back slightly

The lower lip may hang loosely

Dozing

Horses are able to sleep standing up. They can lock one or both of their stifle joints to keep themselves upright. As a horse goes to sleep, its eyes will half close and its head will sink down a little. When horses are in a group, one of them usually stays awake grazing whilst the others doze off in this way.

The foot is tilted, with just the toe touching the ground

Resting a hind foot

Many horses rest a hind leg. This is done not to take weight off the foot (most weight is taken on the front feet) but perhaps to relax the stifle-locking mechanism. If a horse often rests one leg, take note if it rests a different leg, because this may indicate pain.

Rolling around

Usually a horse rolls until its legs are vertical in the air, then back down on the same side, several times. It may even roll right over.

Getting up

A horse gets up front legs first. Its priority is to get its head up high so that it can see if any danger has appeared.

Shaking the dust off

Finally, a horse usually gives a good shake, to remove any excess dust that was picked up during rolling.

THE HERD

A herd of wild horses will include animals of both sexes and all ages. In a domestic situation, geldings (castrated male horses) and mares can be mixed in a field, but this is more likely to lead to fights about leadership, so they tend to be segregated. Stallions are usually kept away from both mares and geldings. It is natural for stallions to collect and mate with mares and fight other male horses. Within any group there is a hierarchy and each horse is responsible for protecting those lower down the order.

Safety in numbers
Horses prefer to be in a group with other horses, even those they do not know. This impulse is so strong that horses that have lost their riders will gallop with the others on the racecourse or in a group out hacking, and single horses grazing may make determined efforts to escape and join horses that pass nearby.

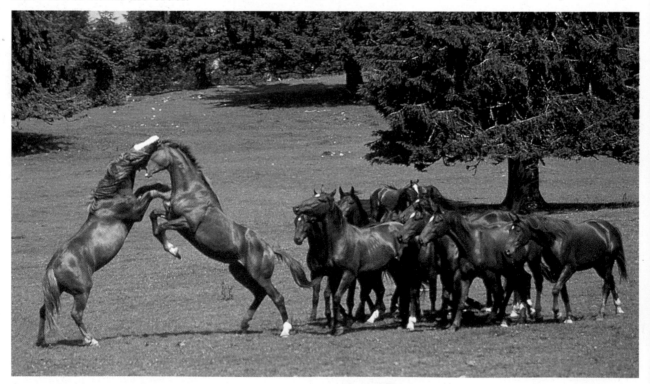

Fighting
Most fights between horses are triggered by a need to preserve a particular position in the hierarchy, or a desire to challenge another horse and perhaps gain a higher position. As a result there is much ritual posturing rather than serious physical damage.

A fight will take on a new intensity when a stallion has collected a harem of mares and is challenged by an outsider. As a general rule, though, horses are not aggressive; where instinct is concerned, they prefer "flight" to "fight".

Arguments

Even in a group of only mares or only geldings, there will be horses that establish dominance within sub-groups. A dominant horse will try to bring more members of the herd into their group, so arguments may occur between group leaders.

Caring for young

The herd is an extended family, and many members contribute to the care and education of foals. Young horses naturally gather together and the nearest adult will usually act as "nanny", even if it is a gelding. This is not as altruistic as it seems – all the adults want to establish dominance over the young ones, not just the dams.

Friendship

Some horses within a group may develop strong attachments to each other. When they are stabled, this can mean that if only one horse is taken out for a ride then the stay-at-home friend becomes very upset. If two good companions are turned out together, they will usually stay fairly close to one another. If one of the friends dies or is sold, the remaining horse may show all the signs of grief.

Rounding up

In a herd, stallions round up their mares. This is to ward off the slightest sexual threat from a rival stallion, rather than to protect the mares from danger. In many domesticated groups, horses of either sex will round up horses that they dominate as part of their efforts to reinforce that dominance.

Chapter 2

GENERAL CARE

WILD HORSES have considerable tactile and social contact with other horses, but domesticated horses often have very little. A domesticated horse needs contact with people instead, and this is given through activities such as grooming and exercising. Stable management tasks may be boring for you, but do not aim to complete them as quickly as you can; they are interesting diversions for the horse. Stabled horses with no stimuli may develop harmful habits because they are bored.

OWNING A HORSE

When you decide to own a horse, it means you are accepting full responsibility for the horse's welfare. To fulfil your obligation, you must understand the horse's needs, both mental and physical. Ignorance of these can lead to you abusing the horse, albeit unintentionally. Owning a horse is a financial and time-consuming commitment. Budget for one-and-a-half times what you think it will cost; you will need to spend money when the horse needs veterinary attention, or new clothing or shoes, not just when money is available.

THE HORSE'S NATURAL INSTINCTS

Nourishment
One of the horse's natural instincts is to eat and drink. Food and water provide the horse's body with the things it needs to function. To obtain enough nourishment from its natural food of grass, a horse needs to spend most of the day grazing. In the wild, it will eat the food around it and then move to a new area to find more.

Survival
When a zebra runs from a lion it is using its natural instinct to survive by running from danger. Horses have the same instinct and it is strong even in domesticated horses. Do not be surprised, therefore, if a horse tries to run from something that has scared it.

Reproduction
Another instinct of the horse is to reproduce. Even when a domestic mare or stallion is not being used for breeding, its reproductive system is still active. Mares come into season for five days every three weeks in the summer, ready to breed. A mare may become temperamental and more difficult to handle when it is in season.

THE HORSE'S BASIC RIGHTS

Companionship

The horse is a herd animal and needs companionship. If you keep a horse on its own, then you must provide the physical contact and mental stimulation that it would normally receive from other horses in a herd.

Food

A domesticated horse depends entirely on its owner for food. If you expect your horse to work, then you may need to give it food other than just grass or hay.

Careful treatment

A horse may accept orders even from children because it accepts being dominated by a human, as it might be by a member of a herd. There is no need to make a horse submit to you from fear.

YOUR COMMITMENT

Hard work

Keeping a horse involves hard work such as mucking out, carrying hay and water, and grooming. A stabled horse needs exercise every day and a grass-kept horse must be checked twice a day, especially in bad weather.

Expense

The expense associated with keeping a horse is not optional. Food, rugs, farriery, vet visits, and a field or stable are necessities.

KEEPING A HORSE HEALTHY

It is better to prevent disease than to have to treat it once it occurs. Horses can be vaccinated against specific diseases, such as tetanus and equine influenza, but the best general disease prevention is good stable management and a keen eye for deviations from normal health. You must get to know what is normal for your horse. Give it a mini health check once a day; then you will spot a problem if it occurs. Be extra vigilant if your horse has mixed with strange horses, at a show for example, and consider isolating it from other horses when you get home, in case it has picked up an infection.

Signs of health
You should visit a horse at grass twice a day. Check that its feet are in good order, that it does not have any cuts or injuries, and that any rug is in place and not rubbing. If possible, bring the horse in during really bad weather.

Disinfecting the stable
Never introduce a new horse to a dirty stable. The stable should first be cleaned thoroughly and then disinfected. Dirt, especially faeces, renders many types of disinfectant inactive, so disinfection on its own is not an alternative to cleaning – it is a vital element of it.

Check the colour of the eye and mouth membrane

Feel the legs for signs of inflammation

Pick out the feet several times a day

Checking all over
Every day, you should run a hand over literally every part of your horse's body. Look for the classic signs of inflammation: heat, swelling, and pain. Naturally, you should be familiar with the size of any existing lumps and bumps on your horse. The skin should be supple and not show any signs of sweating. Horses often rest one leg more than the others, but look out for any variations in this habit.

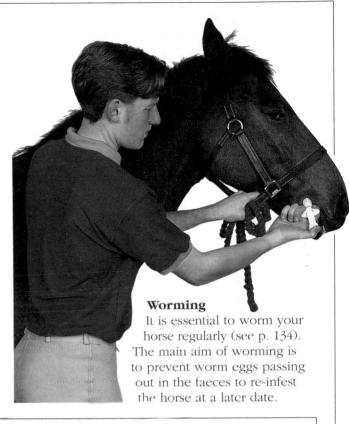

Examining the mouth

Look inside the mouth and make sure that there are no ulcers on the tongue or insides of the cheeks due to sharp points on the teeth. Watch your horse eat. If it drops appreciable amounts of food out of its mouth there may be a dental problem (see p. 129).

Worming

It is essential to worm your horse regularly (see p. 134). The main aim of worming is to prevent worm eggs passing out in the faeces to re-infest the horse at a later date.

CHECKING THE RESPIRATION, TEMPERATURE, AND PULSE

Respiration

A horse normally takes 8–16 breaths per minute while it is at rest. (A breath is counted as one out-in movement of the ribs.) It may be hard to see and count such slow breathing. Stand behind the horse at a safe distance and watch the ribs rise and fall as it breathes.

Temperature

A healthy horse has a temperature of 38.3–38.6°C (101–101.5°F). At first, ask an expert to help you take the temperature. Grease the thermometer with petroleum jelly, shake it hard, then insert it, bulb first, into the rectum, holding on to it tightly. Read the mercury level after about one minute.

Pulse

The normal pulse rate of a horse is 30–50 beats per minute. It takes practice to feel it. Rest the tip of your fingers on the artery that passes over the edge of the lower jaw, and count the beats. Expect the rate to be three or four times the respiratory rate, even after exercise.

HANDLING A HORSE

How you first approach and handle a horse will affect everything else that follows. If you make a horse nervous, it will be suspicious of even the most routine action. Walk up to it steadily, as if you expect it to stand still and wait for you. If it turns away, stand still and wait until it turns around again and is approachable. Talk to the horse all the time, so that it can hear who you are, and reassure it in a friendly tone of voice, rather than issue it orders. Make sure that your movements are smooth and unhurried, so as not to startle the horse. Its natural instinct is to move quickly away from anything that might be dangerous before it stops to think. It will not spend time making allowances for your inexperience or reasoning that you mean it no harm.

APPROACHING A HORSE

1 Approach the horse from the front, at a slight angle from the centre of its head so that it can see you clearly. Make sure that the horse hears you and, when you are close enough, hold out a hand so that it can smell you as well.

Allow the horse to smell and lick your hand

2 Pat the horse gently on the neck. This physical contact is pleasant for the animal and helps to bond it to you. It also shows the horse that you are not afraid of it.

PUTTING ON A HEADCOLLAR

1 Stand at the horse's head, on the near (left-hand) side, and loop the rope over its neck and down the far side. This gives you control over the horse straight away. Most horses will stand still once they feel the rope.

2 Hold both sides of the headcollar, and slide the noseband up over the horse's muzzle. If the horse raises its head, move the headcollar with it so that it stays in position on the nose.

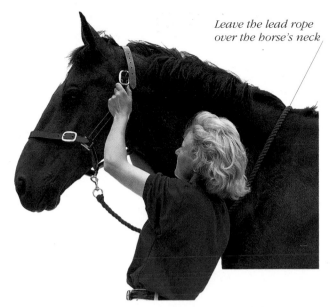

Leave the lead rope over the horse's neck

Use both hands to do up the buckle

3 Use your right hand on the far side of the neck to flick the strap over the horse's poll. Do this calmly. Some horses may be frightened when they feel the strap on the left side of their neck, especially if it is flapped suddenly.

4 Make sure that the strap is fitting snugly just behind the horse's ears before you actually fasten it to the buckle on the cheekpiece. For safety, do the buckle up properly, with the end of the strap tucked in so that it cannot come undone.

5 Finally, check that the headcollar fits correctly and alter the buckles if necessary. Make sure that the clip on the lead rope is facing away from the head, or it may pinch the horse's skin.

THE HALTER

A halter is a type of universally adjustable headcollar. It can be made of webbing or rope. The noseband should lie over the bridge of the horse's nose, with the fastening on the near side of the head. You should always tie the rope with a knot at the side. If you don't, the halter can loosen, in which case it can easily come off over the horse's ears, or it may become too tight.

Correct fit

If the headcollar is too tight it will be uncomfortable; if it is too loose it will not provide safe restraint. The noseband should lie about halfway between the eye and the corner of the mouth, and you should be able to fit at least two fingers under it.

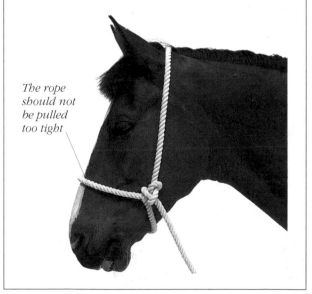

The rope should not be pulled too tight

METHODS OF CONTROL

You will need to restrain your horse for its own good as well as for your convenience. For example, you may need to put on a dressing, check its teeth, or give it worm paste. You cannot expect it to understand when and why you want it to stand still. A horse's natural reaction to anything unexpected or unpleasant is to move away. Therefore you must apply enough restraint to control the horse without causing it pain. If physical means fail, your vet will be able to sedate the horse for a short period using drugs.

WHY CONTROL?

Effective control
A domestic horse must learn that it cannot get its own way by rearing or kicking. If it achieves its aim once, it will use the same tactics in other situations. Use brain rather than brawn to control it. It is probably bigger than you and is certainly heavier. In trials of strength, your horse will win every time.

TYING A HORSE UP

Tie the rope to a loop of string fixed securely to a ring

Using a headcollar
The simplest form of restraint is a headcollar and rope. When you tie a horse up, tie the rope to string, which will break if the horse pulls back in fright. This will stop it panicking even more.

Quick-release knot
You should always use a quick-release knot when you tie a horse up. If the horse gets into any difficulties, such as trapping a leg in a badly positioned haynet, then it is important that you can release it quickly. Quick-release knots are easy to undo, even if the knot has been tightened by the horse pulling backwards.

1 Thread the rope through the string and form the loose end into a loop.

2 Make another loop with the loose end and thread this under and through the first loop.

3 Leave the second loop hanging, then tighten the knot securely by pulling it, and the rope attached to the horse, at the same time.

Untie the knot by pulling the loose end

OTHER METHODS OF RESTRAINT

Distracting with food

During simple, painless tasks, you may be able to distract your horse with food. A haynet is best because it will keep the horse occupied for a reasonable length of time.

Fitting a lungeing cavesson

A lungeing cavesson may be useful in controlling a fractious horse. It looks rather like a sturdy headcollar, but the long lunge rein is attached on top of the horse's nose rather than under its jaw. This makes it easier to stop the horse rearing.

The noseband should be well padded and fit the horse snugly

Hold the foot up so that all the leg joints are flexed

Lifting a foot

Lifting up a foot may help to restrain your horse if you are doing something to one of the other legs. Horses can stand comfortably on three legs, but take care because some will stand on two legs and kick with the third leg.

Twisting the skin

Stallions grasp a fold of skin to restrain mares. You can use the same technique by twisting a handful of loose skin on the horse's neck.

Using a humane twitch

As a final resort, a twitch applied to the top lip can make a horse oblivious to unpleasant stimuli. It causes the release of endorphins, or natural painkillers, into the bloodstream. Always use a rigid metal twitch; a rope twitch can be twisted too far and can cause rope burns.

Apply a twitch for only a few minutes

LEADING IN HAND

A well-behaved horse can be led safely, even past traffic, although this is not a natural form of behaviour for it. A horse has to learn how to be led every bit as much as how to jump. Most horses learn when they are foals, but you must be prepared for a horse to revert to its natural instinct of flight at any time. It is traditional always to walk on the near side of the horse, because most people are right-handed, and this means your strongest arm is next to the horse. Practise leading on both sides, however, so that the horse gets used to it. If the horse is used to being led only from the near side, it will have to learn as if from scratch when you find you have to lead from the other side.

LEADING IN A HEADCOLLAR

Walk at the horse's shoulder; if you walk in front and pull, or stare it in the face, the horse will resist

Holding the rope
Hold the lead rope 30–45 cm (12–18 in) from the headcollar with one hand, and hold the end off the ground with the other hand. You will then have more chance of holding on if the horse suddenly pulls away from you. Never wrap the rope around your hand. If the horse bolts you will not be able to release yourself, and you may get seriously hurt.

LEADING IN A BRIDLE

More control
A bridle gives you more control than a headcollar. When leading a horse in a bridle, bring the reins over the horse's head and hold them in the same way that you would hold a rope. Do not loop the reins around your arm or wrist.

Leading on the road
Always use a bridle when leading a horse on the road. Walk in the same direction as the traffic, putting yourself between the horse and the traffic. This means you may have to lead from the off (right-hand) side. If the horse sees you there, it is less likely to mind the traffic.

TURNING ROUND

1 Being a large, four-legged animal, a horse needs more space to turn than a human being needs. It cannot "about turn" like a soldier. When you turn a horse, steady it first, then turn its head away from you, keeping yourself on the outside of the circle.

The hindquarters should not swing out, because this unbalances the horse

When you turn you should always be on the outside of the horse

2 As you turn the horse's head away from you, the horse will have to bend its neck, and you will then not have to pull it round.

3 During the turn, you will inevitably move slightly in front of the horse's shoulder. Once the turn is completed and the horse is walking in a straight line, position yourself correctly again.

CHECKING A HORSE'S FEET

There is a well-known saying: "no foot – no horse". The vast majority of lameness problems have their origin in the feet (see p. 122), so anything that has a harmful effect on the feet is painful for the horse and reduces its ability to work. You need to check all four feet daily: This includes picking them out, looking for injuries, and checking that any shoes fitted are not loose. The feet must be checked regularly by a farrier and trimmed if necessary, whether or not the shoes are worn out. If a shoe comes off, arrange for the farrier to come as soon as possible. Never work a horse with only three shoes; it is better to remove the shoe on the other side to keep that pair of feet level.

NEGLECTED FEET

Signs of neglect
On neglected feet, the hoof walls start to crack and break away at the bottom. The walls splay out, becoming concave. Some problems, such as laminitis or a sudden change in diet, result in horizontal ridges in the hoof wall.

LIFTING A FRONT FOOT

1 Stand close to the horse's shoulder, facing the tail. Place the hand nearest the horse on the animal's shoulder, and move it down towards the leg. This lets the horse know that you are about to pick up its leg, so it will not get a fright.

2 Reach round the back of the horse's leg, then run your hand down the inside. Keep a light but firm pressure on the leg.

3 Press backwards and upwards on the back of the pastern to encourage the horse to lift its foot. If it does not, grip the pastern and pull the foot up and back.

4 When the horse lifts its foot, support the leg by putting your hand around the hoof wall, with your palm against the inside wall. If you need to examine the foot or use a hoof pick, tilt the sole up.

LIFTING A HIND FOOT

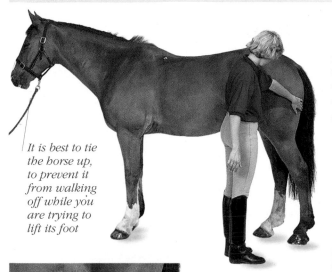

It is best to tie the horse up, to prevent it from walking off while you are trying to lift its foot

1 Stand close to the horse; then, if it kicks, it will hurt less because the leg will have built up little momentum. Run your nearest hand down the horse's hindquarters.

2 Bring your hand around to the front of the leg just below the stifle. Then run it down the inside of the lower leg, maintaining a light but firm pressure.

Bend your knees to avoid straining your back

3 Take hold of the back of the fetlock. Squeeze it gently, and pull the joint upwards and forwards. This should encourage the horse to lift its foot up off the ground.

4 Raise the foot so that it is well clear of the ground, but do not hold it up too high or you will unbalance the horse and cause it discomfort. Hold the foot steady by putting your other hand around the toe whilst you release your grip on the fetlock.

5 Support the leg by taking hold of the toe of the foot from the inside with your original hand. Let the foot rest in your palm. You cannot tilt the foot as much as a front foot.

USING A HOOF PICK

Pick out the feet at least twice a day, and check the foot at the same time for any disorders. Choose a hoof pick that is not too sharp. Clean the grooves beside the frog first, then the sole of the foot. Always work towards the toe to avoid damaging the frog or the horse's leg, should the pick slip. Remove all mud and debris and any flaking horn.

HORSESHOES

Horses were not designed to travel long distances. Wild horses spend most of their time grazing, moving on only to find food or to escape danger. Domestic horses are asked to cover relatively long distances, often on hard roads. Their hooves cannot take the wear and tear, so iron shoes are used to protect them. Horses that are not worked regularly on hard ground may not need shoes. Seek expert advice if you are considering working a horse barefooted.

SHOES AND NAILS

Types of shoe
Ready-made shoes come in different sizes for different sizes of horse. Most shoes have a groove in the underside, called fullering, to make them lighter and to give better grip. Non-fullered shoes are called plain-stamped. A horse's shoes should always suit its planned activities.

Fullered shoes

Fullering

Nail hole

Nails

Nails come in sizes to match shoe sizes, and the correct size must always be used

Plain-stamped shoe for slow work

"Circular" front shoe

"Diamond-shaped" hind shoe

STUDS

Studs are used in pre-drilled holes in the heel of a shoe to increase grip. A spanner is needed to screw them in tightly. Studs must be removed for work on roads or hard ground, because they tilt the foot and reduce the area in contact with the ground.

Stud hole

Stud

Stud shoe

Tap for cleaning stud hole

SIGNS THAT RE-SHOEING IS NECESSARY

Checking shoes
Look out for signs that your horse needs shoeing before its scheduled time. For example, a shoe may come loose, in which case you will be able to move it slightly with your fingers, a nail might come loose or fall out, or the shoe may be worn. Do not wait until shoes have worn out before you call the farrier. The hooves may need trimming before that.

Heel of the shoe pressing on the frog

Poorly fitted shoe

Worn toe

Shoe that has worn early or unevenly

Risen clench (bent-over nail)

Shoe with loose or missing nails

REMOVING A SHOE

1 In an emergency, when the farrier cannot come straight away, it is better to remove a loose shoe than leave it only partly fastened to the foot and risk it injuring the horse. To remove a front shoe, hold the foot between your knees to leave both hands free. Knock up the clenches using a hammer and buffer (see p. 54).

Don't hold the foot too high so that it is uncomfortable for the horse

KNOCKING DOWN A CLENCH

If you see a raised clench, you may be able to knock it down and keep the shoe on until a farrier arrives. Stand the horse on a hard surface, then knock the clench down with a few firm downward blows of a hammer.

2 Grasp a heel of the shoe with pincers so that the jaws are between the shoe and the hoof. Loosen the shoe with a sharp strong movement towards the toe. Do the same with the other heel.

3 If it is difficult to free the shoe, remove one or more nails. This is easiest with nail pincers, but you can use ordinary pliers. Loosen the shoe gradually down both sides, levering towards the toe.

4 When you reach the toe, remove the shoe completely. Lever it off sideways so as not to split the hoof. Be sure not to leave any old nails on the ground, where the horse could tread on them and injure its foot.

Removing a hind shoe

When you have to remove a hind shoe, hold the leg up over one knee rather than between your knees. Stand with your back to the horse's head, and let the hoof lie on the inside of your knee. Press your side into the angle of the horse's hock to restrict its ability to kick. Remove the shoe in the same way as a front shoe. It is more difficult to hold a hind leg than a front leg, and the procedure does take practice.

SHOEING PROCEDURE

Arrange to have your horse shod regularly. On average, a farrier will need to visit every four to six weeks. Even if the shoes are not worn out, the hoof will have grown and will need trimming. Having your horse shod properly is expensive, but do not leave the shoes on in an effort to save money. Badly fitting shoes are painful for the horse and can cause permanent damage. Shoeing can be carried out either hot or cold. In hot shoeing, the shoes are heated so that the farrier can shape them to fit the feet. In cold shoeing, only small alterations to the shape of the shoe are possible. Never be tempted to do the shoeing yourself, even just replacing a nail. Shoeing is a skilled craft which, for the horse's sake, should be left to farriers.

FARRIERS' EQUIPMENT

Some of a farrier's tools are specialist tools, used only for shoeing. A pritchel is used to carry a hot shoe from the forge to the horse. Clenching tongs are used to bend over the trimmed end of the nails, called clenches, to hold the shoe in place. A buffer is used with a hammer to knock up the clenches when removing a shoe. A drawing knife is for paring and trimming the foot and the frog.

Pritchel

Buffer

Double pritchel

Clenching tongs

Pincers

Nail puller

Hoof cutter

Hammer

Drawing knife

Rasp

HOT SHOEING PROCEDURE

1 After removing the old shoe, the farrier's first step is to pare away all the loose flakes of horn from the sole. This enables the length of the hoof wall to be assessed in relation to the sole.

2 The appropriate length of wall is then trimmed off using the hoof cutters. The aim is to return the hoof wall to the length it was when the horse was last shod. More horn usually needs to be removed around the toe than around the heel, because this area grows quickest.

3 The uneven surface left by the small bites of the hoof cutters is filed level with a hoof rasp. It should not be necessary for the farrier to file away significant amounts of the wall at the toe. Too much filing is called "dumping".

4 The shoe is heated until it is red hot and then shaped by hammering it against an anvil. The shoe will need to be returned to the furnace to re-heat it during the shaping process. Hammering iron that is not hot enough weakens the metal.

5 When the shoe is ready, the farrier holds it gently in position against the hoof. This is not to burn a seating for the shoe but to discolour any proud areas of horn, which would prevent the shoe fitting properly. These areas are then rasped level.

6 When the farrier is satisfied, the shoe is cooled in water and nailed in place. There is no definitive number of nails which have to be used, just the fewest possible needed to keep the shoe secure – traditionally four on the outside and three on the inside.

7 The ends of the nails are twisted off and bent over with the clenching tongs, to form clenches. The farrier will usually rest the horse's foot on a special tripod. This makes it easier to form the clenches because it frees both hands to use the tongs.

8 The foot is finished off. Sharp edges on the clenches are rasped away, and the hoof wall is rasped lightly where it meets the shoe. This is to reduce the risk of the hoof cracking, not to make the foot fit the shoe. Any clips are tapped gently into place.

SIGNS OF GOOD SHOEING

The final result

Good shoeing produces a symmetrical hoof, with the inside and outside wall the same length. The edge of the shoe should follow the wall of the toe. The heels of the shoe must be long enough so that all the bottom of the hoof is protected. A shoe can be slightly larger than the hoof – the hoof will spread to fit it. It must never be smaller than the hoof. Ask someone to recommend a good farrier. Proper shoeing takes time. The best farrier will probably not be the quickest or the cheapest.

Clenches about one-third of the way up the wall

Frog and sole are trimmed neatly but not excessively

Heels are protected by the shoe

Clenches are in a straight line and not through the old holes

Shoe is flush with the hoof

Toe is not dumped

Toe clip fits neatly into the hoof

Nails are the correct size to fit the shoe

GROOMING EQUIPMENT

A grooming kit is not a random mixture of brushes, but a collection of specific grooming tools. Each one is designed to do its job without hurting the horse's often sensitive skin. If you use the wrong piece of equipment at any stage you could hurt the horse, and if a brush does not do its job properly you will be wasting your time. A grooming kit should be kept clean, because any dirt from an implement may be brushed into tiny cuts in the skin and subsequently cause infection.

Individual kits
Each horse should have its own, labelled grooming kit. This prevents diseases such as ringworm being spread from horse to horse. There are a variety of proprietary boxes in which you can keep a grooming kit.

You could use a household plastic tray for a grooming kit

Stiff synthetic bristles

Soft fibre bristles

Metal curry comb
This curry comb should never be used on the horse. It is used only for cleaning the body brush (see p. 59). Keep it free of hair to maintain its effectiveness.

Body brushes
These brushes are used to remove dust and scurf from a stabled horse's coat. They have short, closely spaced bristles. Body brushes vary in stiffness. The finer the horse's coat, the softer the brush should be. You should also use a softer brush on a summer coat than you do on a winter coat, because the coat will not be so thick.

Curry combs
Plastic and rubber curry combs are used for removing dirt, especially dried mud from grass-kept horses. They can be used directly on the horse, although care should be taken when using them on horses with a thin coat or sensitive skin.

Plastic curry comb

Rubber curry comb

Cactus cloth
This can be used dry or damp to remove dried mud or sweat. Soak it before you first use it, to soften it.

Dandy brush

This is the first brush to use on a dirty coat. The bristles are long and well spaced compared to the body brush. Do not use a dandy brush on sensitive or clipped areas of the body.

Water brush

This can be used to lay a mane and tail (see p. 61). It is also useful for removing difficult stains from a pale-coloured coat. Use it slightly damp, not soaking wet.

Hoof pick

A hoof pick must have a blunt end. If the point is sharp it could cut the sole of the foot, or puncture the sole if the horse treads on it. A hoof pick is a vital grooming tool. Keep it where you will find it.

Sponges

You need two soft, good-quality sponges – one for the eyes, nose, and mouth, and one for the dock region under the tail. Do not use a perished sponge, because this might result in bits of sponge getting into the horse's eyes.

Massage pad

This is used on a clean, working horse, to help develop the muscles and stimulate the blood supply to the skin. This massaging is called wisping (see p. 60).

Stable rubber

Usually made of linen, a stable rubber can be used to give the coat a final polish. It should be washed regularly.

MAKING A WISP

Traditionally, wisping, or massaging, is done with a wisp made from straw or hay. To make a wisp, dampen some straw or hay and twist it into a "rope" 2–2.5 m (6½–8 ft) long. Make two loops at one end of the rope, one slightly bigger than the other. Wrap the long end in tight figures-of-eight around the loops down to the end. Twist the rope through the end of each loop, and tuck the end in securely.

Make the loops the size you want the wisp – it should fit comfortably in your hand

Make the twists as tight and as neat as possible

Tuck the end into the wisp

Hoof oil

Hoof oil can be clear or black. You can brush oil on clean, dry hooves to protect them and to enhance their appearance (see p. 61). Applying hoof oil does not improve the quality of the existing horn.

GROOMING A HORSE

Wild horses survive perfectly well without being groomed but domestic horses are expected to be free from mud, stains, and dust. Grass-kept horses should not be groomed excessively because the grease in their coat helps to keep them warm and dry. Just pick out their feet and remove mud and stains, especially from areas where tack will lie. A full grooming of a stabled horse is called strapping. It removes dirt and massages the muscles and skin, stimulating the release of natural oils into the coat and improving the circulation. It is most effective when done after exercise, when the horse is warm. Most horses enjoy being groomed but some are ticklish in places. If possible, groom outside, so that the dust and hairs blow away and are not just redistributed.

GROOMING FOR COMFORT

Mutual grooming
Horses will groom each other with their teeth to form social bonds as well as to provide a welcome scratch. They will also roll in dust, as a form of dry shampooing, and rub against trees, which is the equivalent of being brushed.

QUARTERING

Give your horse a quick groom before you exercise it in the morning, to make it comfortable and tidy. Pick out the feet, sponge the face and dock, brush the coat lightly, and remove major stains with a sponge or water brush. This procedure is called quartering, because a horse that is rugged-up is done a quarter at a time with the rug folded back or forwards.

REMOVING MUD

1 Start by picking out the feet. Pull the hoof pick down each side of the frog from heel to toe to remove manure or mud. You may also need to run the pick around the inside of the shoe.

Using a rubber curry comb

Using a dandy brush

2 Remove dried mud with a rubber curry comb or dandy brush. Use them in a straight line, following the lie of the coat. The dandy brush is relatively harsh, so avoid using it on tender parts such as the belly and clipped areas, or on a thin coat.

USING THE BODY BRUSH

Flip the mane to the other side

1 After removing mud, use the body brush to clean and massage the skin. Start along the crest of the neck, brushing in the direction of the lie of the coat with short circular strokes. Press hard so that the bristles reach right down to the skin.

Cleaning a body brush
Keep the body brush clean with a metal curry comb. After every four or five strokes, push the bristles across the curry comb. From time to time, tap a corner of the curry comb on a hard surface, away from the horse, to dislodge dirt.

2 When you have brushed the crest of the neck thoroughly, flip back the mane and work on it a few locks at a time. Use your fingers to remove any tangles, then brush the mane down the neck from the roots downwards.

Be careful not to pull the hairs as you untangle them

3 Brush all parts of the body, working towards the tail. When you brush sensitive areas, such as the inside of the legs and the groin, stand close to the horse and to the side so that it cannot kick you.

4 Finish one side, then do the other. Use the left hand on the left side of the horse and the right hand on the right side. Put your weight behind the strokes. If you do not get tired you are probably not being vigorous enough.

5 Dispense with the curry comb for grooming the face. Untie the horse and hold the rope while you groom with a soft brush. Move the headcollar or take it off and buckle it around the neck, so that you can groom underneath the straps.

BRUSHING THE TAIL

Removing tangles
Untangle any knots with your fingers then brush the tail with a body brush. Take care not to pull hairs out and never use a dandy brush or curry comb on the tail. Hold the tail in one hand, and shake a small section free. Brush this with long flowing strokes starting at the bottom. Brush in more hairs bit by bit until you have done all the tail.

WISPING

Start with five bangs on each area and increase the number gradually

Toning the muscles
Wisp only the neck, shoulders, quarters, and thighs to tone the muscles. Bang the wisp or pad down with reasonable force and make a short stroke in the direction of the coat.

SPONGING THE EYES, MUZZLE, AND DOCK

The eyes
The sponge should be damp, but not wet enough to release water into the eye. Do not attempt to open the eye; the idea is to clean the eyelids. Start at the outside corner and sponge inwards, so that you do the dirtiest part last.

The muzzle
Sponge around the lips, then sponge the nostrils. You can put the sponge right into a nostril to clean inside it. Then remove any discharges from the outside.

Lift the tail out of the way

The dock
Use a different sponge for the dock area. Gently sponge the underside of the dock, and the whole area under the tail.

LAYING THE MANE

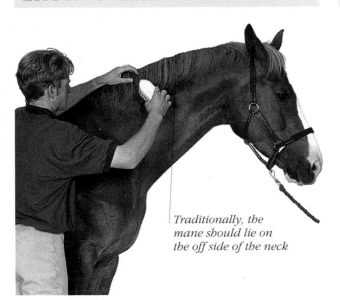

Traditionally, the mane should lie on the off side of the neck

Flattening the hairs
Laying the mane encourages the hairs to lie flat and look neat. Wet the water brush and shake it once to remove excess water. Place it on the base of the mane and brush from the roots downwards.

LAYING THE TAIL

Tidying the tail
Lay the top of the tail with a water brush in the same way as the mane. Pay particular attention to the short hairs, which would otherwise stick upwards. When you have finished the tail you can bandage it to keep it tidy (see p. 174).

USING A STABLE RUBBER

Place your free hand on the horse, in a non-ticklish area

Polishing the coat
Slightly dampen the stable rubber and fold it into a flat pad. Wipe all over the body in the direction of the hairs to remove any remaining dust.

OILING THE HOOVES

Brush any mud off the hooves before applying oil. In muddy conditions it may be necessary to wash them. If you do wash the hooves, dry them thoroughly or the oil will not be effective. Never apply oil to a dirty hoof, because this will seal in the dirt. Cover the whole hoof, from the bulbs of the heel up to the coronet, with a thin, even coating of oil. Oil the sole of the hoof, too. This will help to prevent mud, ice, and straw from getting packed into the foot.

Use a small, hard-bristled brush

PREPARING FOR A SHOW

Your horse will probably know that it is a special day before it gets to the show, and may well be excited from the moment you arrive at the stable. Its anticipation may be triggered by small changes in routine on previous days, or it may sense your mood. You will have to start early in the morning because there is a great deal of work to be done. There is no point doing this the night before, because the horse may roll and you will have to do it again.

WASHING

Washing the mane

1 Wet the mane thoroughly, using a sponge and warm, not hot, water. Be careful not to get water in the horse's eyes. Do not forget the forelock; bring it back behind the ears to join the mane. Make sure that the water penetrates down to the skin at the roots of the hairs.

Start at the top of the neck

2 Use a mild soap or shampoo to soap the mane. Do not use a detergent. Work the lather well into the base of the hairs, to remove any scurf from the skin. Leave the lather in place for a few minutes.

3 Rinse the mane thoroughly with clean water, then squeeze it out with your hand. Remove water from the neck with a sweat scraper to stop the horse getting chilled.

Washing the tail

You can wet much of the tail in a bucket, but you will need a sponge to wet the top. Do not forget the underneath and make sure that you wash right down to the roots of the hairs. Use several buckets of water to rinse, because it is vital that all the shampoo is removed.

WASHING EQUIPMENT

Shampoo

Bucket

Sponge

Sweat scraper

PULLING

Pulling the mane
Thin or shorten a mane by pulling. Take a few hairs from underneath, wind them around a comb, and pull them out with a sharp tug.

Pulling the tail
Tail pulling can be painful. If you have to pull a tail, take underneath hairs and only a few in a session. You will need to start well in advance of the date of a show.

PULLING EQUIPMENT

Comb

PLAITING

Plaiting the tail
1 You cannot just divide the hairs into three groups and plait, because the hairs grow around the dock. Instead, take a small group of hairs from the centre and each side of the tail at the top.

2 Plait down the tail. Bring in successive groups of hairs from each side and join them into the plait as you continue down.

3 Plait one-third of the way down the tail, then continue without joining in new hairs. Loop the plait under and secure it with thread.

PLAITING EQUIPMENT

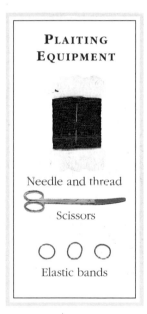

Needle and thread

Scissors

Elastic bands

Make an uneven number of plaits

Plaiting the mane
1 Divide the mane into bunches. Plait each one, joining in a 30-cm (12-in) thread, doubled, a third of the way down. Cut the thread leaving an 8-cm (3-in) end.

Separate the bunches with elastic bands

2 Thread the needle, then wind the thread round the plait and sew the end under. Leave the thread hanging. Follow the same procedure with all the plaits before going to the next stage.

Be careful not to prick the horse with the needle

3 Sew through the top of the plait from underneath to fold the plait in half, and in half again. Pull the thread tight, wind it around the plait, then sew through several times to secure it.

CLIPPING AND TRIMMING

Clipping lets a horse lose more heat during work than it can if wearing its winter coat. If you let a horse sweat too much it will lose condition, and risks getting a chill if it is not dried properly. The clip you use depends on the work your horse does. If it never sweats, then it doesn't need clipping. Few horses like being clipped; all have sensitive areas, such as the belly, and some take time to accept the noise of the clippers. When learning how to clip, ask an expert to show you, and then to supervise you. In any case, you will need a helper to calm the horse. A clipped horse must wear a rug (see p. 168) to replace the insulation you have removed.

THE NATURAL COAT

Winter protection
A horse naturally grows a thick winter coat to protect it against the cold. It is a highly effective form of insulation – more so than many people realize. Snow that falls on a horse's back will not thaw immediately because the coat stops heat escaping from the body.

CLIPPERS

Mains-powered clippers

Tension adjuster for blades

Hole for lubricating oil

On-off switch

Moving blade

Fixed blade

Cleaning brush

Battery-powered clippers

Cleaning brush

Mains-powered clippers
Clippers have two cutting blades. One is fixed and the other moves slightly from side to side – just enough to let hairs enter the channels in the blades. Use clippers that are quiet but as powerful as possible so that they do not get too hot. Check them for electrical safety.

Battery-powered clippers
Most battery clippers are quieter than mains-powered types, so are useful for sensitive or awkward areas such as around the head. They also present no danger of you or the horse tripping over a flex.

USING CLIPPERS

Adjusting the tension
Blades that are too loose rattle and pull the coat instead of cutting properly. If they are too tight, they put a strain on the motor and get very hot. To tighten them, slowly turn the screw. When the noise changes, as the blades stop moving freely, loosen the tension very slightly.

Oiling the blades
Oil the blades every so often while you are clipping, otherwise they will get hot and burn the horse's skin. Turn off the clippers first.

Spray or drip lubricating oil into the hole

TYPES OF CLIP

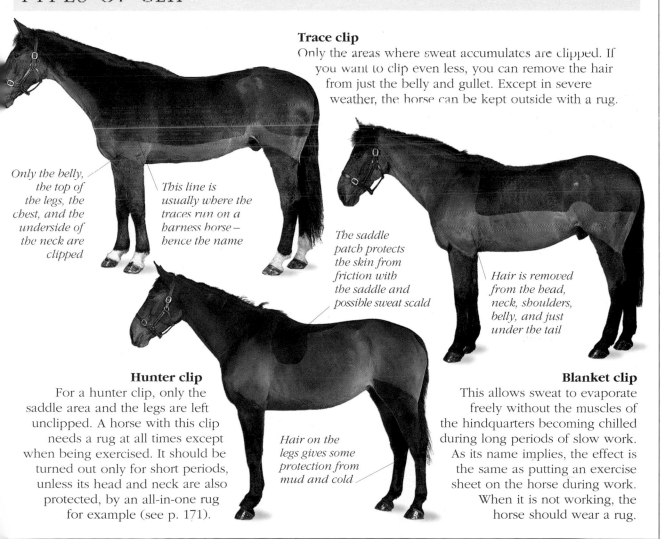

Trace clip
Only the areas where sweat accumulates are clipped. If you want to clip even less, you can remove the hair from just the belly and gullet. Except in severe weather, the horse can be kept outside with a rug.

Only the belly, the top of the legs, the chest, and the underside of the neck are clipped

This line is usually where the traces run on a harness horse – hence the name

The saddle patch protects the skin from friction with the saddle and possible sweat scald

Hair is removed from the head, neck, shoulders, belly, and just under the tail

Hunter clip
For a hunter clip, only the saddle area and the legs are left unclipped. A horse with this clip needs a rug at all times except when being exercised. It should be turned out only for short periods, unless its head and neck are also protected, by an all-in-one rug for example (see p. 171).

Hair on the legs gives some protection from mud and cold

Blanket clip
This allows sweat to evaporate freely without the muscles of the hindquarters becoming chilled during long periods of slow work. As its name implies, the effect is the same as putting an exercise sheet on the horse during work. When it is not working, the horse should wear a rug.

CLIPPING A HORSE

1 Draw the outline of the clip you want with chalk. (This horse will have a blanket clip.) Don't just start work and hope that the clip will turn out symmetrical with straight edges.

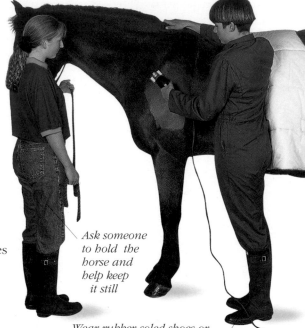

Stand between the horse and the electric flex so that there is no danger of the horse treading on it

Follow the line of the muscles in the leg to make a nice shape

Bandage the horse's tail to keep it out of the way

2 The shoulder is the best place to start; most horses will accept the clippers here. Use smooth strokes against the lie of the hairs. Keep the blade parallel to the skin. If you tilt it down it will nick the skin, and if you tilt it up it will not cut well.

Ask someone to hold the horse and help keep it still

Wear rubber-soled shoes or boots for safety when using mains-powered clippers

If a helper is not holding the horse, tie the horse up, preferably with a haynet to keep it occupied

3 In certain places the skin is very loose or, because of the shape of the body, the area to be clipped is concave. These places can be difficult to clip neatly without nicking the skin. The solution is to stretch the skin with your other hand so that you are still clipping a firm, flat surface.

4 A similar difficulty arises with the elbow. Ask your helper to hold the leg up in a flexed position. This will pull the skin tight and enable you to clip it. Clipping around the "armpit" may be ticklish for the horse, so be ready in case it flinches and jerks its leg.

TRIMMING

Ears

Hold the ear with one hand so that the two edges touch each other, then trim the hairs that stick out beyond these edges. Use scissors with rounded ends. Never cut the hairs inside the ears; these protect the inner parts from dirt and infection. Cut upwards away from the horse's eye to avoid the risk of the points going in the eye if the horse moves its head.

Face

Long hairs under the horse's chin and lower jaw should be trimmed with scissors, but not the whiskers. These are part of the horse's touch apparatus. Lift the hairs to be cut with a comb so that no whiskers are included.

Tail

Tidy the bottom of the tail by cutting across, parallel to the ground. When the horse is carrying its tail properly, the end should be a hand's width below the hocks.

Ask someone to hold the tail up over one arm so that it hangs as it would when the horse is moving

Heels

You may need to trim the feathers (the long hairs on the back of the leg, the fetlock, and the heel), so that the skin can be easily kept clean and dry. This helps to prevent mud fever. Run the comb upwards through the hair and cut the ends neatly, but not too close.

TRANSPORTING A HORSE

There are two types of purpose-built vehicle for transporting horses by road. A horsebox is really a covered lorry. A horse trailer, as its name implies, is towed behind a car. Some horseboxes can transport 10 or more horses, whereas a trailer can carry only two. In many countries, a special licence is needed to drive a horse box. Ventilation is important; make sure that there is plenty of fresh air flowing through, but no draughts, and whenever you stop, open all the doors and ramps to ensure a full air change. Both types of vehicle need regular maintenance for safety, a fact often overlooked, by trailer owners especially.

Storage space for food and tack

Groom's entrance

Ring for tying up horses

Horsebox

There are a number of points to consider when choosing a horsebox. The vehicle's overall weight may affect whether a special driving licence is needed. The layout may require horses to travel facing either sideways or front to back; both methods have their supporters. Some boxes load at the rear, but others load at the side. Avoid vehicles that have luxurious living quarters for the people but cramped and poorly equipped facilities for the horses.

Trailer

Before attaching a trailer to a car, always check that its laden weight is within the car's safety limit. The car's registration number must be shown on the rear of the trailer. During a journey, the trailer must be hitched as shown here. Never travel in a trailer: it is dangerous.

Front exit

The spare tyre must always be ready for use

The safety catch on the ball and socket is closed

The trailer brake is off

The jockey wheel and any supports are raised

Checklist

Before buying a box or trailer, check that it has suitable fixtures and fittings. You will find it easier to load and unload if all doors, bolts, and other parts are easy to move and not too heavy. The floor should be easy to clean, with good grip for the horse's feet. Do not transport horses at night unless there is a good light inside the trailer for loading and checking during transit.

Rear blinds should be lowered only in very bad weather, because they reduce ventilation

The walls and partition should have some padding on which the horse can lean

The breast bar must be firm when in place, and padded – horses may lean against it during braking

There should be a tape, chain, or bar as a rear restraint for each horse

A front ramp is preferable for unloading

There must be a means by which you can secure the partition during travel

Rear supports are necessary to stabilize a trailer during loading and unloading.

The ramp must have a good surface on which the horse can walk easily

On arrival

When you arrive at an event, lower the rear support on a trailer, and put the brake on. Unload the horses, and walk them around in hand for five minutes. This will loosen any muscles that they were using to brace themselves against movement during the journey. Then tie the horses up outside the vehicle, in the shade. Give them access to fresh water, and provide a haynet if appropriate.

CAREFUL DRIVING WITH A TRAILER

If you have ever tried to travel standing up on a bus without hanging on to anything, you will realize what it is like for a horse to travel. Always think ahead, braking and accelerating gradually. Take corners slowly. Trailers can easily skid when water or ice reduces road adhesion. You should not tow a trailer unless you have practised reversing it, in case this is necessary in an emergency. Stop regularly to check the horses, and check them properly, not with just a quick glance. Never travel for more than eight hours in any one day, even with stops.

LOADING AND UNLOADING

Horses do not naturally enjoy walking into an enclosed space such as a horsebox or trailer. Remain calm and be prepared for the horse to stop suddenly, rear, or go backwards. Use as long a lead rope as possible – you must be able to keep hold of the horse even if the unexpected does happen. A helper makes loading easier and safer, but most horses will go into a box or trailer with no problems if they have travelled before with no ill-effects and have confidence in you.

WHAT THE HORSE SHOULD WEAR

Head protection must be made of dense foam if it is to be effective

A tail guard protects the tail from being rubbed

When preparing a horse for travelling, remember that sudden movements of the vehicle may unbalance the horse. The legs should therefore be padded up to, and including, the knee and hock. The horse's poll should also be protected by thick foam or a poll guard.

A summer sheet protects against knocks, without making the horse too hot

LOADING

Walk confidently up the ramp

The helper should be behind and to one side of the horse, just in its field of vision

1 Approach the trailer from a distance, so that the horse has momentum when it steps on the ramp. Walk in a straight line up the centre of the ramp. If possible, ask someone to walk a little way behind the horse. Once the horse knows that there is someone there, it is less likely to stop. If you have a problem, try attaching a long rope or lunge rein to either side of the trailer and ask two people to cross over behind the horse with the ropes.

2 If a single horse is to travel in a dual-horse trailer, put it on the side nearest the middle of the road, for a smoother ride. Ask your helper to fasten the bar or chain behind the horse and close the ramp once you are inside the trailer. Next, tie the horse up, making sure that the rope is long enough for the horse to stand right against the partition; it may want to lean against it during the journey. You can provide the horse with a small haynet to prevent it from becoming bored during the journey.

UNLOADING

1 If the trailer gives you the option to unload at the front, always use this exit. First remove any equipment that is stowed in front of the horse. (If you do store something here during a journey, make sure that it cannot slide around.) Untie the head, and then remove the breast bar. In vehicles containing two or more horses, unload the horse nearest the ramp first.

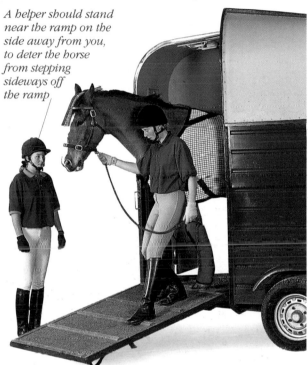

A helper should stand near the ramp on the side away from you, to deter the horse from stepping sideways off the ramp

2 Lead the horse out calmly. Do not let it pull you out. If there is another horse in the trailer, secure the first one, then untie the second, move the partition over to widen the exit, and lead the horse out.

A helper standing to the side of the ramp and slightly away, can help to keep the horse straight

Rear unloading
Unloading from the rear can be difficult. Horses do not move backwards easily, and the travelling boots restrict movement further. Untie the head when you are on the same side of the breast bar as the horse. Ask a helper to undo the rear bar or chain, and be ready in case the horse pulls backwards. Guide the horse out; you cannot expect it to be able to keep itself straight.

THE HORSE AT EXERCISE

The change from rest to full work must be gradual. As a guideline, a horse should spend at least a week just walking, a week walking and trotting increasing distances, and a week introducing canter. To get a horse fit to compete, spend longer on each stage. A change from work to rest must also be gradual. It is bad for a horse suddenly to do nothing.

WARMING UP

Warming up
Before riding, walk and trot a stabled horse up and down in hand a few times, to loosen it up. Ride at the walk and trot for at least 20 minutes before fast work, to increase the blood flow to the horse's muscles. Exertion produces lactic acid, which must be washed away from the muscles as soon as it forms.

AFTER WORK

Cooling off
A horse must be cooled off slowly after hard work. Walk for 10 minutes at the end of a fast hack or other work. Then wash sweat off to make the horse comfortable.

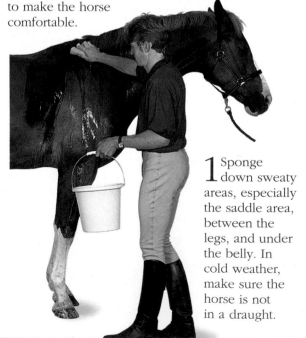

1 Sponge down sweaty areas, especially the saddle area, between the legs, and under the belly. In cold weather, make sure the horse is not in a draught.

FOOD AND WATER

Horses must get used to drinking during exercise. When ridden for long periods they can become dehydrated if the fluid they lose is not replaced. After hard exercise, a horse should be given a little water at a time, to which you can add electrolytes. Do not give a horse a large feed just after work; its digestive system will not be able to cope because the blood will still be concentrated in the muscles.

2 Untie the horse, then move back the headcollar so that you can sponge dirt and sweat away from areas where the bridle has rested. If the horse is tacked up again without being washed, this dirt will rub the skin.

3 Use a sweat scraper to remove excess water. In hot weather, let the horse dry slowly; the evaporation of the water gives a cooling effect.

4 Wash the heels and pasterns and dry them thoroughly with a towel. These are prime sites for mud fever, a painful infection that infiltrates wet skin (see p. 130). White legs are particularly susceptible.

Secure the sweat sheet with a roller

5 Quietly walk the horse around until all sweat or water has evaporated from the coat and the horse is dry. Do not leave the horse standing in a stable when still wet.

It is important to check that the horse has not broken out into a sweat again under a rug

6 In winter, ensure that the skin does not get too cold. A layer of straw under a sweat sheet will keep the skin warm and still let water evaporate.

AT A SHOW

Caring for the horse
Make sure that you warm the horse up adequately before each class. Between classes, do not just tie your horse up and abandon it; check that it is comfortable, has clean water to drink, and possibly a haynet.

Sponging the mouth
At a show, the horse may wear a bit for far longer than normal. Moisten the inside of its mouth with a wet sponge at least before each class.

Cooling off
When you have finished an event, tend to your horse. Walk it around in a sweat sheet to allow it to relax and to make sure that its temperature is stable before you load it to take home.

Chapter 3

THE HORSE AT GRASS

HORSES ARE grazing animals, so an open area of grass is their natural environment. In the wild, they have space to move around and choose what they eat and where they sleep. A horse cannot do this when it is confined to a field, so make sure that the field you provide is safe and attractive to it. Maintaining a safe field, supplying suitable food and shelter, and handling a horse correctly when you turn it out and catch it are all important aspects of keeping a horse at grass.

THE FIELD

Horses are very selective grazers. They graze some areas right down to the soil (the lawns), but leave other areas untouched (the rough) and use them only for dunging. The rough grows long and coarse and becomes infested with weeds. If horses are left on their own to graze a field, the rough gets larger and the field becomes an eye-sore and unsuitable for grazing. The secret of maintaining a good horse paddock is to keep it topped (cut) to the same height, so reducing the distinction between lawn and rough. This topping can be done by other animals, such as sheep or cattle, or by mechanical means. It is best to divide the available area into two or three separate fields and use them in rotation. This mimics nature, and gives you the opportunity to maintain the quality of the grazing.

A tall hedge provides shelter and extra security

The shed is positioned so that a horse cannot get trapped between it and the fence

The access road has a hard, level surface that will remain good in winter

Fresh drinking water is supplied in a trough

Ideal conditions

The grass is of uniform height and weed free

A poisonous tree is fenced off to prevent horses from eating it

The field drains well, away from the gate and the water trough

A suitable field

Try to find a field for your horse that is not too steep. It should not be high up in an exposed location, nor in a low-lying area where it will get muddy in winter. The minimum amount of grazing for one horse is 0.4 hectares (1 acre).

FIELD MAINTENANCE	
Season	**Maintenance procedures**
Spring	Grass growth is at its most rapid at this time and may exceed the horse's ability to eat it, so topping may be necessary. In early spring, some poisonous plants may sprout before the grass and tempt horses, so watch carefully and remove any potentially dangerous plants.
Summer	Grass growth varies greatly with the rainfall. Irrigation may be necessary to help a paddock recover in dry weather before it is grazed again on rotation. Harrowing breaks open dung and reduces worm larvae levels. It may be possible to take a crop of hay off one of the paddocks.
Autumn	The time for boundary maintenance – laying hedges and applying preservative to wooden fences and field shelters. Watch out for acorns and other poisonous fruits and seeds, which may need to be collected to prevent horses from eating them.
Winter	Keep an eye on hedges, which may develop holes when the foliage dies. It may be better to feed hay than to have all the grass eaten early in the season. Watch areas that get poached (cut up and muddy). Take steps, such as moving the feeding points, to stop this from happening.

Unsuitable conditions

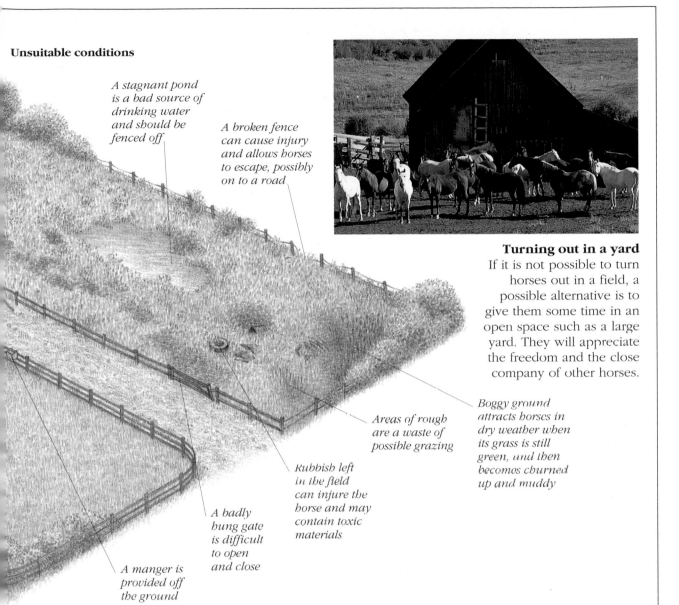

A stagnant pond is a bad source of drinking water and should be fenced off

A broken fence can cause injury and allows horses to escape, possibly on to a road

Areas of rough are a waste of possible grazing

Boggy ground attracts horses in dry weather when its grass is still green, and then becomes churned up and muddy

Rubbish left in the field can injure the horse and may contain toxic materials

A badly hung gate is difficult to open and close

A manger is provided off the ground

Rounded corners help to prevent a horse from getting trapped in the corner and injured when horses gallop around the field together

Turning out in a yard

If it is not possible to turn horses out in a field, a possible alternative is to give them some time in an open space such as a large yard. They will appreciate the freedom and the close company of other horses.

WORM CONTROL

Grazing sheep or cattle with a horse reduces the number of infective worms available to the horse. Worms usually affect only one animal species, and the larvae of worms that affect horses die in cattle and sheep. Topping the grass also helps, because worm larvae move to the top of the grass in order to be taken in by a horse (see p. 134). Harrowing breaks open dung, leaving larvae and eggs to dry up, but it also spreads the larvae slightly. It is better to remove the droppings, and therefore the worm eggs, every week.

FENCING AND GATES

Effective fencing both keeps a horse safe and prevents it from straying. The law in many countries requires owners to use adequate means to contain their horses in a field. The type of fence needed depends on the type of horse. For example, a high single-rail fence that keeps in a 17-hand hunter may allow a Shetland pony to walk underneath. Similarly, a draught horse could just push through a fence that is a formidable obstacle to a pony. A thick hedge is the best kind of fencing, but must not contain any poisonous plants (see p. 84). It also provides shelter from the weather. Remember that a fence can be less effective in winter; snow drifts reduce the effective height, and holes can appear in a deciduous hedge, making it easier to push through.

FENCES

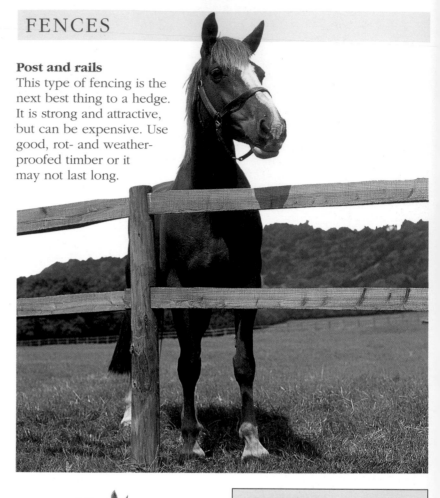

Post and rails
This type of fencing is the next best thing to a hedge. It is strong and attractive, but can be expensive. Use good, rot- and weather-proofed timber or it may not last long.

Plain wire fencing
If it is well built, with the wire stretched taut, a plain round-wire fence may be effective. Use five or six strands, with the bottom one at least 30 cm (1 ft) above the ground. There is a danger that the horse may not notice the strands, and gallop into the wire. Use markers, such as strips of white cloth, to make the wires visible.

DANGEROUS FENCING

Fencing should not rely on pain for its effect. Barbed wire, for instance, may be acceptable for sheep or cattle, but it is not safe for horses, with their fine skin. Every year, many horses sustain a nasty wound from a barbed-wire fence. If a strand breaks, it is very dangerous because it can wrap itself around a horse's leg. A loose strand of any kind of wire is dangerous for the same reason. Wire mesh is unsuitable too, because if a horse puts its foot through the mesh, it may be unable to pull its leg free without sustaining an injury.

Flexi-fencing

This consists of strong plastic tape stretched between wooden posts. It may not look as smart as post and rails, but it is cheaper and can be just as effective. The white tape is also highly visible to the horse. It is long-lasting because it does not rot.

Electric fencing

This is effective, especially if used with another fence. When a horse touches the wire, it gets a small shock. Do not use it with a thin skinned horse, and make the wire visible. The wire is not a good barrier if the current is off. Horses learn that they will get a shock only if they can hear the characteristic ticking.

MAINTENANCE

Check fencing and gates regularly and mend them if necessary before a horse escapes or injures itself. Strands of wire can stretch so they may need tightening. The ends of wooden fence posts, which are buried in the ground, rot faster than the parts above ground so they need checking carefully. Store any spare posts in dry conditions otherwise they will start to deteriorate even before you install them. Paint wooden fences with non-toxic preservative about every two years.

GATES

Wooden gates

Gates should open into the field so that the horse cannot push its way out. Wooden gates are relatively light. Like fences, they need regular painting with wood preservative. It is worth fitting good-quality hinges and fastenings, because these make opening and closing the gate much easier.

Metal gates

Heavy-duty metal field gates are strong and are long-lasting if properly rust-proofed, but they are expensive. Metal gates can be heavy and difficult to handle; in addition, if a horse does try to get over the gate or gets its leg trapped in the bars, it can be seriously injured because the bars do not break.

WATER AND SHELTER

A lack of either clean water or adequate shelter can seriously affect a horse's health. Without water, horses can become dehydrated and die, and hot sun, pouring rain, and flies can be extremely unpleasant for horses and cause skin diseases (see p. 130). Whichever form of water supply or shelter you use, it must cater for all the horses in the field. It must be sited so that no horse can get trapped behind it. Water must be clean and unpolluted from industry or agriculture and, if it is not, it must be fenced off.

WATER

Natural water source
A clean running stream is an ideal water source if the banks allow easy access for the horse. The stream must have a gravel bottom. If it is sandy, the horse may take in sand with the water, which can cause colic. A pond may be suitable if it is fed by a spring, or is large enough to remain clear. Stagnant ponds and drainage ditches must not be used.

Trough and piped water supply
Water troughs should be constructed of non-ferrous metal that will not rust. Ideally, the trough should be fed by water on a demand valve. Flush and scrub it out occasionally, to keep the water clean and fresh. The trough should be sited where the drainage is good so that the surrounding area does not become very muddy, and not under a tree where leaves will fall in it.

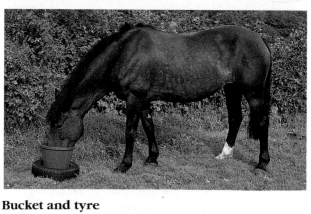

Bucket and tyre
If you use a bucket as a water source, use one without a handle so that the horse cannot get its foot trapped in it. Stand the bucket inside a tyre so that it cannot be kicked over. Buckets must be checked and refilled at least twice a day.

IN WINTER

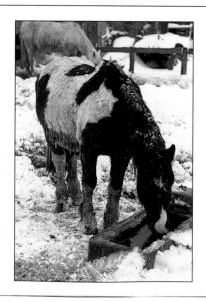

Check twice a day in winter that the water supply has not frozen. This involves more than breaking ice. The feeder valve of a trough, and the supply pipe, can freeze. If this happens, you must provide a different source of water.

SHELTER

Standing together

Horses use each other as shelter from the weather. They often also stand head to tail and use their tail to swish flies away from the other's head. A horse on its own will usually point its rear end towards the wind, because the large muscle masses of its quarters, with their generous blood supply, stay warm more easily.

Trees and hedges

A tree or hedge can provide shelter in summer and winter. Trees provide shade from the sun, and hedges give shelter from the wind. Horses need to be able to stand downwind from a hedge when the prevailing wind is blowing.

Purpose-built shelter

A shed is a good type of shelter. If the floor gets muddy, put down some bedding such as straw. The shed may be used very little. The point of a shelter is that it is there for a horse to use when it decides it needs to. When it does use the shed, you can be sure that shelter was vitally necessary.

The back wall of the shelter should face the prevailing wind

The open front prevents a horse being cornered or injured inside

Open barn

A large barn in a field has the advantage that a number of horses can shelter together and continue their social interaction under cover. The main aim is to provide shelter from hot sun in the summer whilst allowing any cooling breeze to flow through. It will also provide some protection from winter weather. There must be enough room in the barn for all the horses in the field.

GOOD AND BAD GRAZING

Just turning a horse loose in a field of green vegetation does not guarantee that it will get enough to eat. First of all, the nutritional value will depend on which plants are present. A field of thistles is of little use as food. Secondly, it will depend on the state of growth of the plants. Most grasses are at their most nutritious before they go to seed. Finally, it will depend on the height of the grass. Horses prefer to graze shorter rather than longer grass.

GRAZING AREAS

Rough and lawn
Horses prefer areas rich in good grazing plants; these areas become lawns. Areas with unpalatable plants are left as rough. The uneaten plants produce seeds and multiply, making the rough worse.

GOOD PLANTS

Poa annua (Meadow grass)
Sometimes called meadow grass, this used to be common in water meadows in temperate climates. It provides good ground cover, and is enjoyed by horses.

Festuca (Fescue)
Fescue grasses are relatively hardy. They are less palatable to horses than some other types, so may be ignored if horses have alternative species to graze.

Lolium (Ryegrass)
Ryegrass grows quickly. Most seed-mixes for farm use in temperate climates contain a high percentage of it. It is not very drought-resistant, but grows well early in the season.

Phleum pratense (Timothy)
This is not a terribly hardy grass, but is very palatable, and is much sought after by horses when it is present. Timothy is also a tasty and nutritious element in hay.

Dactylis glomerata (Cocksfoot)
The advantage of cocksfoot is its ability to withstand spells of really dry weather during its growing season. It does not have a high carbohydrate content.

Cichorium intybus (Wild chicory)

To human taste, chicory is quite bitter, but it is readily eaten by animals. Wild chicory is nutritious for horses because it has a good mineral content.

Taraxacum officinale (Dandelion)

Dandelions are useful for grazing. Their broad leaves are quite palatable to horses, but a horse will be able to find them only if the grass is short.

Trifolium repens (White clover)

Clover has a high starch content. Unfortunately, because it is so rich it can cause laminitis (see p. 122) to develop, so a high pasture percentage is undesirable for ponies.

BAD PLANTS

Carduus (Thistle)

Thistles are painful to eat, and the spines from the leaves and stems can damage the horse's mouth. Thistles grow tall and spread their seeds well. They therefore multiply easily.

Holcus lanatus (Yorkshire fog)

The plant is not harmful to horses, but it has little nutritional value. It is a nuisance because it smothers other species of grass in a pasture, including more pleasant and nutritious plants.

Urtica dioica (Nettle)

Nettles sting the inside of a horse's mouth, so horses do not willingly eat them. They are a problem because they grow rapidly and can smother more desirable plants.

Agropyron repens (Couchgrass)

This type of grass has a relatively low nutritional value. It spreads rapidly by extending new growth through surrounding vegetation rather than relying on seeds. It can cover and destroy the palatable plants.

POISONOUS PLANTS

Most poisonous plants have an unpleasant taste, but if a horse acquires the taste for a plant it will often go out of its way to find it. Even after several months of stabling, horses may go straight to the plant when turned out again. You must check pastures weekly for any signs of poisonous plants. If the horse gets there before you there may be little to see, so learn to look carefully. It is best to dig up and burn small numbers of plants. Weed killers may be used, but you must usually wait a couple of weeks after applying them before the paddock can be grazed again.

Treating pastures

The more there is of a poisonous plant in a field, the harder it is for a horse to avoid eating it. If the plants are growing when grass is limited, it is tempting for a horse to eat them.

Quercus (Oak)

Oak leaves and acorns are poisonous, probably because they contain tannic acid. They cause constipation and kidney damage.

Laburnum leaves

Laburnum vossii (Laburnum)

All parts are poisonous to horses, especially the seeds, and can kill. Affected horses develop nervous malfunctions, and go into a coma.

Laburnum tree in flower

Senecio jacobaea (Ragwort)

This is toxic even when dried, when it is more palatable. It has a cumulative effect, causing fibrosis of the liver and acute liver failure.

Sorghum vulgare (Sorghum)

This can be harmful due to its cyanide and nitrate content. It can cause breathing problems and death. Young plants are not toxic.

Atropa belladonna (Deadly nightshade)

The plant contains atropine, which dilates the pupils, so this is a symptom of poisoning. Affected horses may be unable to stand.

The deadly nightshade berry is highly poisonous

The shiny yellow flowers may warn animals not to eat buttercups

Ranunculus (Buttercup)

Buttercups are mildly poisonous when they are alive. The plant is not poisonous when it is dried, for example in hay.

Pteridium (Bracken)

This is cumulatively toxic in large amounts and remains so in hay. An affected horse will stand with its back arched and feet apart, growing more and more sleepy.

Oxytropis splendens (Locoweed)

The entire plant is toxic. Affected horses become unpredictable and dangerous and slowly paralysed.

Acer rubrum (Red maple)

The attractive red leaves are poisonous to horses in summer and autumn. Horses become jaundiced and anaemic.

Ricinus communis (Castor bean)

A tiny amount of castor bean is fatal, but its nasty taste means that the beans are usually eaten only by accident.

All parts of yew are poisonous, even when dead

Hypericum (St John's wort)

This causes white skin to become sensitive to light and painfully sunburnt.

Taxus baccata (Yew)

This is the most toxic plant. It causes sudden death – a horse may die with leaves still in its mouth.

Equisetum (Horsetail)

This grows in moist, rich soils. A horse poisoned with horsetail will start to stagger, and after a while fall over.

The leaves have a distinctive, feathery shape

TURNING OUT A HORSE

Putting a horse out in a field not only allows it food and exercise, but also gives it the opportunity for social interaction. It is important that the horse has times when it is its own master, as a contrast to the discipline that you impose. You can learn a lot about a horse's character by watching how it behaves when turned out with others. You can, for example, find out which horses are its friends, which it would like to be exercised with or stabled near, and which ignore or bully it.

GETTING EXCITED

Jumping for joy
Some horses get very excited when they are turned out. Keep an eye on them until they settle down, in case they injure themselves. If you ensure that the horse is hungry when turned out, it may prefer to put its head down and feed rather than gallop about.

MEETING OTHER HORSES

The horse stretches its head forwards, keeping its body as far as possible from the other horse's hooves

Approaching strangers
When a horse greets a strange horse, or one that is not from its close circle of companions, it does so head on. Both horses want to see each other as clearly as possible, and be confident that they cannot be kicked by the other horse.

Greeting friends
When a horse greets a companion, the two animals do not bother to turn and face each other. They will deliberately move close together, often nuzzling each other to provide actual physical contact, and may touch muzzle to muzzle.

BULLYING

Flattened ears show tension

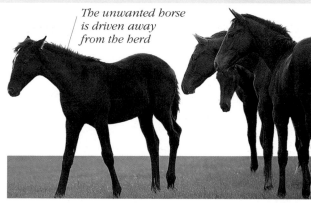

The unwanted horse is driven away from the herd

Displaying dominance . . .

Every herd, however small, has a hierarchy of dominance. Initially, this social order is established by physical threats, biting, and kicking. Afterwards, it is maintained by just body language.

. . . and hostility

Sometimes several horses will pick on a submissive horse and bully it almost constantly without reason. In these circumstances, it is best to remove the victimized horse from that group and try to let it establish itself in another more friendly group. Bullying of one horse by another may represent a fight for dominance in which the bullied horse never accepts the dominance of the other.

SEASONAL NEEDS

Summer

In warm weather, flies can really worry a horse, especially when they land on its head. The flies like to suck moisture from around the eyes; a fly fringe can be very useful for preventing this. The horse soon learns to shake the fly fringe by moving its head.

Winter

Clipped horses must wear rugs for warmth when turned out. Rain and wind are the problems that cause chills, not the actual air temperature. Most horses prefer to be out, well rugged-up, rather than confined to the stable.

Look out for blood or broken skin

Battle scars

Kicking out at another horse is a natural way for a horse to assert or defend itself. Kick injuries can occur out at pasture, especially if the horses are wearing shoes. During your visits to the field, check each horse visually for any injuries, especially any horse standing away from the others. Make sure that you have a first-aid kit available on your visits.

TAKING A HORSE INTO A FIELD

The process of turning a horse out may be daunting for the inexperienced groom. The horse is excited because it is looking forward to its freedom, and doesn't want to delay any more than it has to. At the same time, if you are nervous or unsure of how to proceed, the horse will soon notice. Owners often make life difficult for themselves by not maintaining gates. Opening a stiff gate can require all your strength and concentration, leaving neither for controlling the horse. Often all that is needed is a little oil! It must always be you who is turning the horse out, never the horse turning itself out. If you release a horse just in front of an open gate it may gallop through, but horses can go in reverse too. Never release the horse until both of you are in the field and the gate is shut. You may think you do not need to do the job properly, but it could be disastrous if you don't.

DON'T DO THIS!

Managing two horses
Trying to turn out two horses at once is more than twice as difficult as dealing with one. The horses seem to know instinctively how to go in opposite directions at the crucial moment. It is far better to use one person per horse, or to make two journeys.

CORRECT PROCEDURE

1 Position yourself between the horse and the gate, so that you can control the gate and stop it from hitting the horse. Hold the horse firmly, and unlock or unfasten the gate. Open it wide enough for both you and the horse to pass through easily at the same time.

2 Lead the horse into the field. Don't let it push in front of you so that you find yourself following the animal into the field. Then, while still holding the horse, turn back and close the gate.

3 Lead the horse a good distance into the field, well away from the entrance. If there are other horses in the field, keep your horse clear of them. Turn around so that the horse is looking towards the gate again.

4 Face the horse and take the headcollar off quietly. Hold it and the lead rope carefully, so that you do not frighten the horse. Then pat the horse and step back from it. Do not slap it on the neck or rump, because this may excite it and encourage it to gallop around the field.

5 Once you have turned the horse loose, do not turn your back on it. Instead, walk backwards steadily towards the gate, watching the horse all the time. By doing this you encourage the horse to stay where it is, or move further into the field, rather than follow you towards the gate. It will then be easier for you to open the gate and let yourself out of the field. You will also see if the horse kicks out in excitement and will have a chance to get out of the way.

DEALING WITH A DIFFICULT HORSE

If you anticipate trouble, take precautions. Wear a hat and gloves, and protect the horse by putting boots on it, so that it does not injure itself while galloping about. Never let go of the horse until you are fully in control and well into the field. Use a long lunge rein as a lead rope. This allows you to stand further away from the horse if it rears or bucks, and still hold on to it. Sometimes a horse that is already in the field can cause difficulties when you lead another one in. If this is the case, first go in by yourself, and tip some feed on the ground away from the gate before taking your horse in. This will prevent a dangerous set-to at the gate.

CATCHING A HORSE IN A FIELD

Every horse is born wild. Its instinct is to keep away from potential danger, and that includes humans. To catch a horse in its field, you first have to overcome its basic wariness. It is frustrating to want to go for a ride and not be able to catch the horse. It is also vital that you are able to catch a horse when it needs veterinary care. Unfortunately, some horses associate being caught with an unpleasant experience and are difficult to catch. To cure this problem, catch your horse sometimes just to feed it or talk to it. It will then learn that being caught can lead to something pleasant.

THE BASIC METHOD

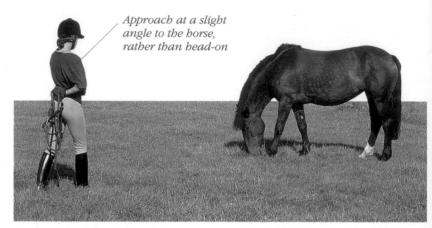

Approach at a slight angle to the horse, rather than head-on

1 Slowly approach the horse from the front and slightly to its left. Hold the headcollar behind your back. Talk to the horse all the time, so that it both sees and hears you. If it first notices you only when you are almost upon it, it may get a fright and its natural instinct will be to move away from you.

2 A horse is naturally curious so it will probably look up as you approach. When it looks at you and acknowledges your presence, stand still and keep its attention until it starts to move towards you. Let it see your open hand and maybe offer it some food. If it moves away, walk around in an arc until you are in the correct position relative to the horse and start the approach again.

3 Let the horse touch you first, possibly to take food from your hand, rather than move your hand to stroke its head or neck. Do not make a grab for the forelock or mane. Bring the headcollar into view slowly so as not to startle the horse. If you lay the lead rope over its neck the horse will probably feel restrained and not move away.

Wait for the horse to come to you before showing it the headcollar

Stand close to the horse while you put on the headcollar

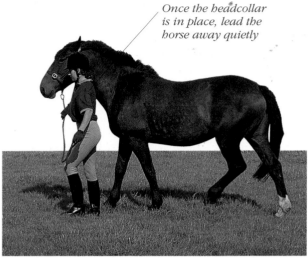

Once the headcollar is in place, lead the horse away quietly

4 Hold both sides of the headcollar and gently raise the noseband until it is in its approximate final position. Keeping your left hand steady, work the headpiece up the far side of the horse's neck in your right hand, and put it over the top of the horse's head. Fasten the buckle, then show the horse that you are pleased with it by patting its neck.

5 Do not relax yet. The horse may still try to pull away suddenly. If it does escape from you, it will be more difficult to catch the second time. Do not wrap the rope around your hand. If you are worried about the horse pulling the rope through your hand, tie a knot at the end of the rope and wear gloves to prevent rope burns to your hands.

CATCHING A DIFFICULT HORSE

Dos and don'ts

Ask someone to help you, then approach the horse from both sides. Do not frighten the horse by moving suddenly or approaching it from behind. If it runs away, do not chase it, but walk up and start again. Never fasten a rope around its neck; if it escapes, the rope could be dangerous. Do not vent your irritation on the horse when you catch it; instead, reward it.

The horse starts to move after its friend as the other horse is led away

1 If your horse is grazing with a companion, the bond between them may be stronger than the horse's desire to avoid being caught. So, if the other horse is easy to catch, catch it first.

2 Lead the other horse away until your horse follows. If possible, ask a helper to catch it. If not, tie one horse up, then catch the horse you really want.

Chapter 4

THE STABLED HORSE

Living in a stable is not natural for a horse. It does not have 24-hour-a-day access to its choice of grazing, which it would have in the wild, and it is separated from other horses against its natural social instincts. If you stable a horse you do it for your own convenience not the horse's, so you must try to provide as good an environment for it as possible. You must consider the psychological amenities that you provide as well as the food, water, and bedding.

THE STABLEYARD

Over the centuries, various ways have evolved to provide stabling for horses. The most common types of stable used today are loose boxes and stalls. Loose boxes are individual "rooms" for horses. These may open to the outside, or may be enclosed in a larger barn. Stalls have solid partitions and, at most, a single bar across the front. They are relatively narrow, but the horses are usually tied up and do not turn around. They are useful for large numbers of placid horses, such as draught horses, but not suitable if the horses are stabled for 24 hours a day.

Site and buildings

The ideal yard has covered areas for horses, feed, tack, and storage and other uses. It is built on two or more sides of a square, with the back of one part facing the prevailing wind so that the yard is sheltered. The site should be level; if it slopes, the lowest point must be free from buildings to ensure good drainage. There must be easy access to paddocks.

A burglar alarm should be fitted where it can be heard by plenty of people

The feed store should have a lockable door wide enough to admit a wheelbarrow, and a properly protected rodent baiting point

A light that comes on automatically at someone's approach is a useful security item and helpful to you

Gates should be in good repair and shut at all times, so that if a horse escapes from its stable it will be confined to the yard

The stable and yard must have proper drainage leading well away from the yard, not based on surface run-off alone

There should be a readily available supply of fresh water and a hose

A clear, covered area is useful for tasks such as clipping, grooming, and dressing wounds

A fire extinguisher is vital, and should be of a type suitable for electrical fires

The tack room must be dry, large enough for tack cleaning, and fitted with locks for security

American barn

In this type of stabling, loose boxes face each other across a central aisle, with the whole area covered over. This provides stimuli for the horses, who can see and talk to each other and see what is going on. Disadvantages are the common air space and ventilation problems, which allow infectious diseases, especially respiratory diseases, to spread rapidly.

Lights must be covered, have animal-proof switches, and be controllable from the main entrance

An area, preferably covered, should be set aside for forks and brooms where they can be tidied out of harm's way immediately after use

Muck heaps should be downwind of the stables and away from the rest of the yard, to keep smells and flies away and to reduce the risk of fire in the yard

The surrounding floor area should be concrete, which cannot become muddy

Health and safety

The stableyard should be kept clean, not just to make it look attractive, but for health and safety reasons too. Rotting dung, urine, and bedding are health hazards to horses and can make the yard slippery and dangerous. In case of an emergency, such as fire, make a list of the procedures to be followed and put it where it can be seen easily. You should also write the vet's telephone number where you can find it quickly when you need it.

THE STABLE

When a horse is put in a stable it cannot choose when or where to find shelter, or when and what to eat and drink. You must therefore take full responsibility for all aspects of its daily life. It is unfair to house it in a stable with dangerous fittings that may cause injury, or in one with such poor ventilation that the horse develops respiratory problems. Even though the horse is in an unnatural environment, you should try to make it as happy as it would be out in a field. If a horse is stabled full time it can become bored, so make sure that it can see what is going on around it.

The size of the stable

The minimum size for a horse's stable is usually 3.6 m (12 ft) square and 2.7 m (9 ft) high. The sides should be at least one-and-a-half times the horse's length.

The floor must be hard-wearing, impervious to moisture, have a non-slip surface, and should slope gently for drainage

Window

Windows are a source of light, as well as part of the ventilation system. In many cases they do not need any glazing, merely window bars. If you do wish to glaze them, consider using Perspex-type materials rather than glass, which is dangerous if it is broken. Louvre openings may be better than a single opening.

INTERNAL FITTINGS

Tie rings
These should be fixed firmly – one at the horse's ear height for a haynet, and one lower down for tying up the horse.

Water bucket
If possible, hang this on a wall. If it is on the floor, it can be knocked over or get full of bedding.

Manger
This should be fixed so that the top is at the horse's natural nose height. The corners should be rounded so that food does not lodge there. Anti-spill bars across the top are useful.

Air vent

There should be an air vent near or in the roof of the stable, to make air flow around the stable and then be pushed out by fresh air coming in through the door. The vent should not be fitted where it just causes a draught.

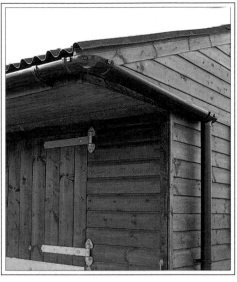

Roofing material must not be too noisy when hit by rain or hail, and must not become too hot in direct sunlight

The doorway should be at least 1 m (3½ ft) wide and 2 m (7 ft) high

The horse must be able to move around and lie down

The bottom door should be at least 1.2 m (4 ft) high

Overhang and drainage

It is important that the stable roof has efficient guttering, and that captured water runs into a drain or large water butt. If it does not, the stableyard can become a muddy mess as horses and people walk through the puddles. There should be an overhang on the roof, to protect the horse and its bedding from the rain, which might otherwise blow in through the open door.

Hook on door

The top stable door should always be left open but never left to swing loose, because it could hit the horse's head. It should be hooked back.

Horse-proof bolt

The bottom stable door must have fastenings at the top and the base. The top bolt needs a safety device, because some horses learn to open other bolts.

The safety catch of this horse-proof bolt has to be held up to allow the bolt to be slid open

Kick bolt

The bottom bolt braces the door against any kicking by the horse. A kick bolt is opened with the foot. It enables you to open the door with one hand without bending down, which is useful if you have a heavy bucket or are leading a horse.

BEDDING MATERIALS

Clean, warm bedding is essential for any stabled horse. Bedding provides comfort and insulation, prevents a horse's feet from being jarred by standing for a long time on a hard surface, and encourages a horse to pass urine and droppings. The most important factor when choosing a material to use as bedding is the comfort of the horse. Other considerations, such as the cost, how clean it keeps the horse, and how easy it is to deal with and dispose of, must be regarded as secondary to the horse's needs.

COMFORT

A bed to lie on
Although horses are able to sleep standing up, they like to lie down from time to time. If a horse does not have adequate clean bedding, it will hurt its joints when lying down. This can lead to a capped hock or elbow (see p. 125). Wet bedding feels cold, and can scald the horse's skin.

STRAW

Advantages and disadvantages
Straw, the traditional bedding for horses, is widely available in temperate climates, and fairly cheap. Often, however, it is full of fungal spores, which can trigger respiratory problems (see p. 139). Barley straw is the most widely used. Wheat is good, especially if it has long stems. Oat straw is the least common type, and is quite harsh and prickly.

Oat straw is absorbent

Oat straw

Dusty bedding
The dust particles seen in a stable containing straw are too big to get into a horse's lungs, but a large amount may be a warning that fungal spores, which cannot be seen with the naked eye, are present. Straw usually contains some fungi, and any plant-based material can become infested if left as deep-litter bedding.

Barley straw is yellower than other straw

Wheat straw drains best

Wheat straw

Barley straw

OTHER BEDDING MATERIALS

Shavings
Wood shavings are now readily available as bedding. They are easy to muck out if you have the correct equipment (see p. 100). Clean, dry shavings are a good form of bedding for horses with respiratory problems. The main drawback is that disposal may not be easy, because shavings take time to rot down.

Newspaper
Shredded newspaper, packaged in bales, can be bought fairly cheaply. It is rather like sterile straw when first put down, so can be useful for horses that are allergic to straw. However, once it gets wet with urine it starts to disintegrate and is rapidly invaded by fungi. Disposal of the waste may be a problem.

Hemp
This is a relatively new bedding for horses, and not as widely available as others. It is made from the core of the stem of a non-narcotic hemp plant. It rots down more easily than shavings, does not degenerate as much as paper when wet, and absorbs a lot of moisture. It should be dealt with like shavings (see p. 102).

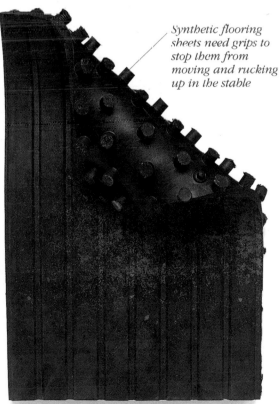

Synthetic flooring sheets need grips to stop them from moving and rucking up in the stable

Rubber flooring
Porous rubber bedding sheets drain well, so form a dry floor. On the other hand, they provide little comfort for the horse, and because droppings lie on the surface, they can easily dirty the horse's coat. This type of material can be useful in a trailer or horsebox, where a horse does not lie down.

Sand
Sand might be considered the natural bed for Arabs and other horses that have a desert origin. It makes a dry bed which moulds well to the horse's shape. It is also cool, which is useful in hot climates. It is not organic, so it is not likely to cause respiratory problems. It is important not to give food on the floor; the horse can ingest sand with it and this may result in colic.

MUCKING OUT

Wet bedding, droppings, and urine fumes are unpleasant for the horse, so must be removed as quickly as possible. A stable should be cleaned out once a day, and if a horse is stabled all the time, droppings must be removed and the bedding levelled out and made comfortable at least three times a day. If the bedding is always damp it can cause infections, especially of the foot. Thrush, an infection of the frog (see p. 123), is a particular danger. Dirty bedding also inevitably leads to a dirty horse, which makes grooming more difficult. The "deep litter" system, in which fresh bedding is added to existing bedding, and the stable is cleared out only every few months, should be avoided. The bedding will store fumes and fungal spores, and these can affect the horse's health.

TOOLS

Mucking out used to be done with only a fork, a shovel, a broom, and a wheelbarrow. Now there are extra tools to cope with bedding other than straw, and to save time and effort. A shavings fork is essential for beds of wood shavings; it allows clean bits to fall through the small gaps, while catching droppings and any wet material held together by damp. There are also "hods" you can use to collect droppings and lift them easily into a skip or wheelbarrow.

Fork   Shovel   Broom

Shavings fork

Wheelbarrow

Hod

Small rake

Skip

DEALING WITH DIRTY STRAW AND DROPPINGS

1 First remove any visible droppings with a fork. Search carefully, because some may be covered with straw. Lift each pile with some straw underneath the droppings.

2 Tip the droppings into a skip, keeping as much clean straw as possible. A plastic basket like the one shown here is a good, cheap substitute for a purpose-made skip.

3 Separate the clean and the dirty (or wet) straw. Toss the clean straw to the sides of the stable, leaving the dirty straw on the floor.

Most horses will usually dirty the straw in the same place in the stable

4 Load all the dirty straw into a wheelbarrow. Try to avoid pushing dirty straw into the clean straw.

5 Toss the clean straw up into the air and against the wall, forming a pile along the wall. This fluffs it up and allows any further hidden droppings to fall out. Try to pile the straw against two different walls each day. This ensures that each part of the bank (see p. 102) is broken up every other day.

Toss the straw to break it up so that it makes a comfortable bed

6 Brush the remaining dust, droppings, and dirty straw into a pile in the centre of the stable, ready to remove. Leave the rest of the floor as clean as possible and the clean straw piled up along the stable walls.

7 Using the shovel, lift the pile of dirty material into the wheelbarrow.

PUTTING DOWN THE BED

1 Leave the stable to air and dry before you put the bed down. Toss the old straw on the floor, leaving enough by the walls to form a bank around the walls (see step 2). Add fresh straw to replace what you removed. Mix the new straw in with the old if your horse tends to eat it.

Use the fork to toss the straw in the air to fluff it up, then spread it on the floor

2 Use the remains of the piles of old clean straw to form an even bank of dense straw all around the stable. This will help to prevent the horse from getting cast on its back if it lies down or rolls close to the wall. Work backwards around the stable, using the fork to push the straw firmly up against the wall, then level the top.

3 When straw is well shaken up it can look thick, but will soon be compacted by the horse. To test if the bed is thick enough, drop a fork into it. If you hear its tines hit the floor, you need more straw.

MUCKING OUT SHAVINGS

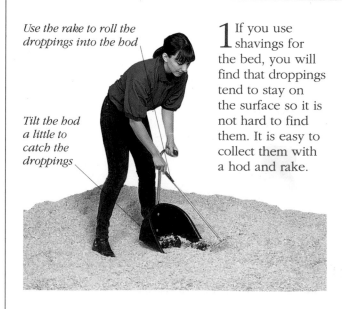

Use the rake to roll the droppings into the hod

Tilt the hod a little to catch the droppings

1 If you use shavings for the bed, you will find that droppings tend to stay on the surface so it is not hard to find them. It is easy to collect them with a hod and rake.

2 Use a shavings fork to sift the bed for droppings and wet shavings, and to fluff it up. High banks may not be needed; unlike straw, shavings will not move around a lot when the horse is lying down.

MUCKING OUT WITH THE HORSE

Using a barrier across the door

If you cannot turn the horse out while you muck out its stable, fix a wooden bar across the doorway. This will stop the horse escaping, and will allow you to duck quickly underneath to enter or leave.

Stay clear of the horse while you work

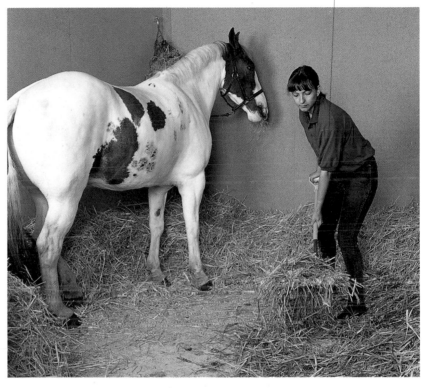

Moving the horse

Use the tools away from the horse so that you do not risk injuring it. Do not work around the horse's feet. Move the horse to one side and then the other while you do each half of the stable.

THE MUCK HEAP

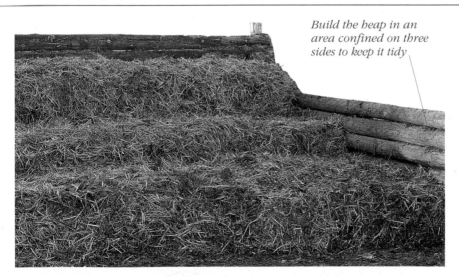

Build the heap in an area confined on three sides to keep it tidy

Store droppings and soiled bedding tidily, in an area accessible to vehicles for disposal. Make the heap in layers so that it is easy to build and allows the rain to penetrate and aid rotting. Spread a layer of muck over the area and compress it by treading it down. Start a second layer at the back, using a plank on top of the first tier to support the wheelbarrow. At a convenient stage, start a third layer. Complete the layers bit by bit, treading them down as you go.

Chapter 5

FOOD AND WATER

A DOMESTICATED horse has a greater range of food available to it than a wild horse has, but it is important to remember that it is still a grazing animal. Whatever else it eats, it should have access to roughage such as grass or hay for most of the day. There are many myths that have grown up around feeding a horse, and you should know the facts behind them. Some lead to regimes that are harmful. How you feed a horse will affect its health, behaviour, and performance. Follow the basic rules of feeding, but do not stick rigidly to formulas. Each horse is an individual, and you must learn what is best for your own.

HOW TO FEED A HORSE

Horses are naturally grazing animals. They cut the grass with their incisor teeth, and chew it with their molar teeth, producing saliva while they chew. The food is mixed with the saliva and swallowed, then it passes into the stomach. The stomach is designed to hold only small amounts of food. This means that a horse doing strenuous exercise may be unable to eat enough grass or hay at one time to replace the energy it has used. By feeding small amounts of "concentrated" feeds (see p. 110) this problem can be overcome. Concentrates provide more energy for a given volume of food than grass or hay.

METHODS OF FEEDING

Loose on the ground
Giving food on the ground allows a horse to eat in a natural way, as if it were grazing on grass, but it is wasteful. The food is mixed with soil and spread out so thinly that the horse cannot pick up all the individual pieces. Another disadvantage is that the horse may pick up silt or sand with the food, which can cause colic.

In a bucket on the ground
A bucket keeps food together, making it easier to eat. Keep one bucket per horse, and use ones without a handle so that a horse cannot get its foot trapped. In a field, put the buckets well apart, so that horses do not try to eat from each other's. Horses with breathing problems should always be fed with their head down. This lets mucus drain out of the respiratory system and not down into the lungs.

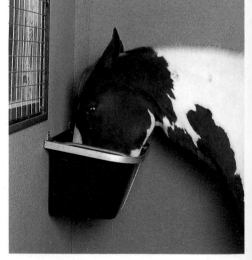

In a manger
Feeding in a manger ensures that the horse cannot spill all the contents, as it could by kicking over a bucket. It also stops a stabled horse from playing with the container if it becomes bored. Another advantage of a manger in a stable is that it leaves more floor space.

RULES FOR FEEDING

Feeding rule	Reason
Always make any feeding changes gradually.	This allows the digestive system to adjust. It applies to new batches of hay and new brands of a feed, as well as to changes in food type – even grass.
Never increase food in anticipation of the work the horse will do.	Feed more concentrates because the horse has lost weight, rather than because you might want to increase its workload in the future. An imbalance between food and work can lead to azoturia or lymphangitis (see p. 137). Reduce feed before reducing a horse's workload, not after.
Feed only good-quality food.	Cleanliness is a reasonable guide to quality for concentrated feeds. If feeds are dull and dusty, their nutritional value will be low. It is not so simple with hay; good, nutritious hay may be a health hazard because of the high number of fungal spores it contains.
Allow the horse access to roughage of some sort for most of the day.	The horse's digestive system is designed to deal with almost continuous amounts of roughage. Its stomach is not designed for large meals.
Always feed by weight rather than volume.	Feeds vary in their volume for a given weight, so a scoop of one feed is not the same weight as a scoop of any other (see p. 110). Each type of feed also varies in its volume for a given weight with every batch you buy.
Do not disturb or work a horse during or immediately after feeding, and do not feed a horse immediately after work.	The blood supply to the horse's muscles is increased during work; therefore that to the digestive system must decrease, causing faulty digestion. Also, if alarmed, a horse may swallow food before chewing it and colic may follow.
Feed concentrates in small amounts at the same times every day.	This evens out the workload of the horse's digestive system, reducing the risk of colic. Feed at regular intervals, not just when it is convenient.
Make clean water always available, but do not let a horse drink too much straight after a feed.	Hay and concentrates are drier than grass. They must be mixed with water in the stomach before digestion, but not washed straight through.

CHECKING A HORSE'S WEIGHT

Measure the girth just behind the elbow, where the saddle girth usually sits

How to find out the weight of a horse

Use the horse's weight to assess the effects of your feeding and exercise regime, not to decide how much to feed. Using a weighbridge is the ideal way to weigh a horse, or you can measure the horse's girth with a weigh-tape, which gives the likely weight. You could also use an ordinary tape measure to find out the horse's girth and length (from the point of shoulder to the point of buttock), and calculate the weight in pounds using the formula below. (To convert to kilograms, multiply the pounds by 0.45.)

Weight (lb) = girth² (in) x length (in) ÷ 300

NUTRITIONAL NEEDS

Each horse has an individual genetic body structure that determines factors such as its height and shape. It has an individual metabolism that determines how well it digests its food, and how efficiently it absorbs nutrients. Each horse also has its own collection of bacteria in its colon to digest roughage. Therefore, the same amount of food will have a different effect on different horses. Feeding guidelines are provided here, but feed your horse according to its needs, not to a formula. Each horse's needs will vary depending on whether it is stabled or kept in a field, whether it is clipped or not, and what the weather is like. If a horse lacks nutrients, one sign is it will lose weight. Ask the previous owner how much they fed the horse, to give you an idea how to start.

PARTS OF A BALANCED DIET

Part of diet	What it does	Where it is found
Protein	Proteins are the body's building blocks. Muscle is mostly protein; tendons and ligaments also have a high protein content.	Most horses' needs are met by grass in summer, and hay (as needed) in winter. In horse cubes, good sources include soyabean.
Carbohydrate	The source of energy, carbohydrates are stored as glycogen in the muscles, ready for instant use during exercise.	Grass or hay gives enough for maintenance but usually not for work. Cereals, such as oats, are the major energy source.
Fat	Fats or oils are a valuable energy source because they can be broken down to simple, easily utilized carbohydrates.	Many ready-mixed feeds include vegetable oils. Up to 15% of a horse's energy needs can be efficiently provided by vegetable oil.
Water	Much of the horse's body contains built-in water; it is the main medium for carrying substances around the body.	Spring grass may have a high water content, but most of a horse's needs are met by drinking. Water must be clean and fresh.
Minerals	Bones obviously need minerals, but most of the body tissues have some mineral requirements.	Alfalfa is a rich source. Minerals are taken in with soil during grazing. Salt can be given as a salt lick.

BULK/CONCENTRATES RATIO

Food and work
Even a horse in hard work should be fed mostly roughage, but grass and hay cannot usually supply all the energy a horse needs for work. The digestive system cannot handle the bulk needed, so extra nutrients are fed as concentrates. However, you must feed according to what your particular horse needs. Some ponies and horses do not need extra concentrates, even when they are working.

Work

Maintenance (no work)
Feed usually no concentrates, just good-quality roughage to maintain normal weight.

Light work
Up to an hour per day of walking with some trotting. Feed up to 15% concentrates.

Medium work
Includes some jumping, cantering, or galloping. Feed up to 30% concentrates.

Hard work
Two hours per day including galloping, or competing. Feed up to 45% concentrates.

Food per day

Roughage

Concentrates

SPECIAL NEEDS

An obese horse *A very thin horse*

Extremes of condition

Over- or underweight

If a horse is over or underweight, do not alter its diet suddenly. It is particularly harmful to put a fat pony on a crash diet because its digestive system will not cope. As a guide, you should be able to see where the ribs end but not see the shape of each individual rib.

Feeding in winter

A stabled horse may not need any more food in winter than in summer. A horse living out will use more energy for warmth in wet and windy weather, so must have extra concentrates. It may also need folic acid supplements to make up for the lower level in grass.

OLD HORSES

In old age, horses may benefit from processed roughage such as chopped straw or complete horse cubes, because lost and long teeth may reduce their ability to deal with hay. They need protein to replace muscle tissue broken down by metabolic ageing, rather than carbohydrates for energy. If the horse is working, frequent, regular feeds will maintain the energy levels.

PLANNING A DIET

Providing energy

When mixing feeds, first decide what work the horse will be doing; that tells you how much energy it must have. You can then combine any feeds that in total will provide the energy, and is concentrated enough for the horse to be able to eat all of it in one day. In equine nutrition, energy in food is usually expressed as megajoules (1 million joules) in a kilogram (2lb 3oz). (1 joule = 0.239 calories)

Energy value of feeds

- Oats: 13.5 megajoules/kg
- Maize: 16.1 megajoules/kg
- Barley: 15 megajoules/kg
- Sugar beet: 12.2 megajoules/kg
- Bran: 11.1 megajoules/kg
- Ready-mixed food – see packet

A GUIDE TO THE ENERGY NEEDS FOR VARIOUS TYPES OF WORK		
Exercise	500-kg (1100-lb) **riding horse**	300-kg (660-lb) **family pony**
Extra 1 hour walking	5 Mj of energy needed on top of maintenance needs. Feed: 0.4 kg (14 oz) sugar beet; *or* 0.3 kg (10½ oz) maize; *or* 0.15 kg (5¼ oz) maize and 0.2 kg (7 oz) sugar beet.	3 Mj of energy needed on top of maintenance needs. Feed: 0.25 kg (8¾ oz) sugar beet; *or* 0.27 kg (9½ oz) bran; *or* 0.1 kg (3½ oz) oats and 0.12 kg (4¼ oz) sugar beet.
Extra 30 minutes trotting	10 Mj of energy needed on top of usual needs. Feed: 0.75 kg (26½ oz) oats; *or* 0.5 kg (35¼ oz) sugar beet and 0.25 kg (8¾ oz) maize; *or* 0.52 kg (17½ oz) oats, and 0.27 kg (9½ oz) bran.	6 Mj of energy needed on top of usual needs. Feed: 0.45 kg (15¾ oz) oats; *or* 0.5 kg (35¼ oz) sugar beet; *or* 0.22 kg (7¾ oz) oats, and 0.27 kg (9½ oz) bran.
Extra 10 minutes galloping	8.33 Mj of energy needed on top of other needs. Feed: 0.5 kg (18½ oz) maize; *or* 0.6 kg (21 oz) oats; *or* 0.2 kg (7 oz) oats, 0.25 kg (8¾ oz) sugar beet, and 0.24 kg (8½ oz) bran.	5 Mj of energy needed on top of other needs. Feed: 0.33 kg (11½ oz) barley; *or* 0.31 kg (11 oz) maize; *or* 0.13 kg (4½ oz) barley and 0.24 kg (8½ oz) sugar beet.

CONCENTRATED FEEDS

There is a large variety of concentrated feedstuffs available. These include proprietary mixes, which can be loose or processed into cubes, and the cereals. Commercial mixes provide a balance of nutrients which your own mixture is unlikely to do. All concentrates are unnatural to the horse, but they provide energy and variety. You must not guess how much feed to give your horse. Do not go "by the scoop", because different feeds weigh different amounts. Many also vary in their volume per unit weight from batch to batch. Each of the feeds shown here is the same weight – 595 g (1 lb 5 oz).

DIFFERENT FEEDS

Bran
Use bran as a bulk food, not as a source of nutrition. It is not good for growing horses because it has too much phosphorus and not enough calcium.

Flaked maize
A valuable feed, maize is often processed further by food companies to make it "non-heating" (not liable to make the horse excitable). The nutritional concentration is lowered so that it provides less energy.

Cubes
There are different cubes, or nuts, to suit different horses, such as "horse and pony" and "racehorse". Buy the right kind for your horse.

Coarse mix
This looks more appetizing than cubes, but a more valid reason to feed it is that it takes longer to eat, which is better for the horse's digestion. It comes in different grades.

Linseed
Uncooked linseed is poisonous. It must be boiled for many hours until the seeds have split. It is a laxative, and it may also help to produce a shiny coat.

Alfalfa pellets
Even in this dried form, alfalfa contains good concentrations of the vitamins and minerals found in grass. It is especially valuable for its calcium and fibre content. It has been called "pelleted sunshine".

Oats
The popularity of oats is mostly due to the fact that careless changes to the quantity fed make little nutritional difference because it has a low energy content. It is not a natural food for horses.

Barley
This is often underrated, but it has a high energy content. Take care when feeding it, because even a small change in the amount fed can have significant nutritional consequences.

Sugar beet pulp
Sugar beet is a valuable feed because it is rich in energy and protein. Pulp is dried beet and must be soaked before feeding.

595 g (1 lb 5 oz) sugar beet pulp weighs a total of 2.6 kg (5 lb 13 oz) after soaking

Sugar beet cubes
Like sugar beet pulp, cubes expand rapidly on contact with moisture, such as saliva, and can cause choking and colic if not soaked first. Never confuse them with ordinary cubes.

Soaked sugar beet
Soak sugar beet for about 12 hours in sufficient cold water so that at the end of that time there is still some water that has not been absorbed.

SUPPLEMENTS

Roots and fruit

Carrots and apples probably top the list of healthy treats for horses. Carrots may be fed in large quantities, but do not have great nutritional value. Cut them lengthwise. Square or round pieces can get stuck in the throat and cause choking.

Cod-liver oil

This is a rich source of vitamins. It can be mixed with food to help condition the coat.

Molasses

A palatable supplement, this is a useful binding agent to add to dry or dusty food. It can also be mixed with medicines and put directly into the horse's mouth.

Corn oil

Oils are a rich source of energy. They can be added to the diet of competition horses, which might be unable to eat enough food to supply their energy needs.

STORING FOOD

Keep feeds in a metal or plastic bin to protect them from insects and rodents – and from your horse. Horses need good-quality food, so never buy more than two to three weeks' supply at a time because it will deteriorate, especially in hot, humid weather. Empty a bin completely before you add more food, or you will end up mixing stale food with the new.

Salt

A salt lick is the best way to supply salt. The horse can have a lick whenever it feels that it needs some.

SOURCES OF ROUGHAGE

The fibrous, bulky part of a horse's diet is called roughage. This may be fed fresh, as grass, or it may be preserved, like hay and silage. The horse's digestive system, unlike that of humans, can obtain nutrients from the plant fibre because it has a very long colon, which has evolved over millions of years for this task. Cellulose, the main component of roughage, is digested in the colon by bacteria that exist in harmony with the horse. The bacteria provide soluble carbohydrates, fatty acids, and amino acids for the horse, in exchange for the chewed-up cellulose on which they live. If a horse does not eat enough bulky food to keep the colon fairly full, colic may result.

Natural food

Grass is the most natural form of roughage for a horse. The horse has to bite off each mouthful, so it eats slowly. Grass changes its character and nutritional value through the seasons. It is most nutritious in early summer, just before flowering. In spring it has a high water content, while in winter some grass is as dry as hay.

HAY

Good hay

Hay is dried grass. Meadow hay, shown here, is made from permanent pasture and contains a variety of grasses and herbs; seed hay is made from specially grown grass. Good hay is crisp, smells sweet, and is greenish brown in colour.

Poor-quality hay

Bad hay will contain more stalk than leaf. It may be yellowish brown in colour rather than green because the pigment has been bleached out. If the hay has been made or stored badly, white mould may even be visible.

This poor-quality hay is brown; it looks dull, in contrast to the springy, glossy appearance of good hay

DANGERS OF BAD HAY

It is important to feed good-quality hay. Some hay may have little nutritional value; some may contain a high concentration of fungal spores which can trigger respiratory ailments. Be sure not to feed hay containing poisonous plants. They can cause death, even when dried.

OTHER FIBROUS FOODS

Vacuum-packed grass
This preserved grass is damp and softer than hay. Horses usually enjoy it, and it has about twice the nutritional value of hay. The grass is vacuum-packed just after harvest, and a cold fermentation then takes place in the bag.

Alfalfa
A good mineral source, alfalfa is fed as hay, or chopped and dried. Its leaves are larger than those of other grasses; this helps to make it more nutritious than the best meadow hay. It is very rich, so feed less of it than you would hay.

Silage
A moist, acid-smelling feed, silage is grass that is compacted and put through a hot fermentation to preserve it. If made in polythene-wrapped bales, it must be stored carefully; badly stored bales have been blamed for equine botulism.

Chaff
To make chaff, straw is chopped into tiny pieces. Chaff can be readily digested by bacteria in the colon, so it should not cause impactions of the bowel as long straw may do. It may be mixed in with concentrated feeds; it has little extra nutritional value, but adds necessary bulk.

HYDROPONIC GRASS

Hydroponic grass is grown artificially on trays that contain no soil. The horse is presented with a mat made up of intertwined seeds, roots, and early shoots. Grass grown in this way has very little fibrous content – less than ordinary grass – but it has a good nutritional value compared to most types of dried roughage.

Chaff and molasses
These two feedstuffs can be mixed to make a feed that is very palatable to most horses. The molasses also binds the chaff together, slightly increases the nutritional value, and makes it less dusty. The feed can be bought pre-mixed, which saves time but may be expensive; it could be cheaper to buy the chaff and molasses and mix them yourself.

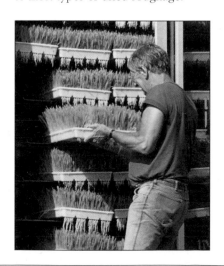

FEEDING HAY

The most natural feeding position for a horse is from the ground. You can feed hay loose on the ground, but much of it will be trampled on and soiled, and therefore wasted. The easiest way to feed hay is in a haynet or hayrack. Divide the horse's daily ration into four roughly equal amounts. Give them at regular intervals, with one first thing in the morning and one last thing at night. When you receive a new batch of hay, keep it separate. Start to feed it gradually over several days, mixing the new hay in with the old. The horse's digestive system can then adapt to the new hay slowly.

FILLING AND WEIGHING A HAYNET

Filling a haynet
Nets made from synthetic twine are best because they do not rot and so last longer. Loosen the drawstring to open the net, then push the hay inside. If you want to make it easier for the horse to pull the hay out, shake it a little to loosen it.

Use your foot to help keep the net open

Weighing a haynet
Weigh the net on a spring balance to ensure a constant level of feeding. A haynet filled with slices of hay straight from the bale will contain much more than one filled with loose hay.

Estimating weight
A hay bale will break easily into equal slices, so you can estimate how much you are using. It is useful to weigh one bale from a new batch, because they vary in size from different batches.

PREVENTING RESPIRATORY PROBLEMS

Good hay

Bad hay

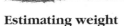
Fungal spore

Fungal spores
Hay contains microscopic fungal spores. It is these, rather than the visible dust particles, that trigger respiratory problems. These greatly enlarged photographs of hay show how bad-quality hay can have a large number of these harmful spores.

Soaking hay
Some of the dust and spores in hay can be washed away by soaking it. Spores also stick to wet hay, and are less easily breathed in by the horse. Immerse the hay in running water for about two hours – no longer, or you may wash out nutrients.

TYING A HAYNET

1 Pull the opening of the haynet shut, then thread the loop of cord through a ring on a wall, a tree, or another suitable place. Whether it is being hung up in the stable or outdoors, a haynet must be hung well clear of the ground. The ring should be just above the horse's eyes.

Thread the cord through one of the mesh links

2 Pull the net up, then thread the cord through the bottom. This helps to compact the net when you tie it up. It also keeps it off the ground when it has been emptied. The net will hang down lower when it is empty, and a horse could get a foot caught in it.

Tuck the remaining cord inside the net so that it is not left hanging

3 Pull the cord tight, bringing the bottom of the net up as high as you can. Tie the cord tightly at the top, using a quick-release knot (see p. 46). Make sure that the loop is not too small.

Turn the knot to the back

4 Finally, turn the haynet around so that the knot is hidden from the horse.

The right height
When you have finished, the haynet should be level with the horse's eyes when it is standing naturally. If the net is lower, the horse may trap its foot in it. If it is higher, dust and seeds will fall in the horse's eyes as it eats.

Hayracks
A fixed hayrack may cost much more to install than a ring for a haynet, but it is easier to fill than a net, and the hay never ends up on the ground. The drawback is that you cannot adjust the height of a hayrack for different horses.

Chapter 6

THE SICK OR INJURED HORSE

Everyone responsible for caring for a horse should know how to look after it in sickness as well as in health. It is a good idea to learn to recognize some of the more obvious symptoms of diseases and disorders, so that you know how to treat them and know when to call for help. If in doubt, call the vet. It is better to be safe than sorry.

POSSIBLE DISORDERS

Many common ailments are linked to domestication. It is not that people knowingly cause disorders but, when things do go wrong, their management practices can make a problem worse. Ailments may arise due to the work that a horse is asked to do – no wild horse repeatedly performs movements, as is necessary in dressage. Some diseases occur when a horse is stabled – chronic obstructive pulmonary disease (COPD) is triggered by mouldy hay or straw. Others can spread through travel. In the wild, equine influenza is usually transmitted only within a herd, but it can spread quickly, even from country to country, when horses mix at competitions.

Warning signs

Inflammation is a symptom of most horse ailments, so you must always be on the lookout for the classic signs – heat, pain, and swelling. Any sudden change from normal behaviour should also set alarm bells ringing. You should rely on noticing that a sign of good health (see p. 28) is absent, rather than try to learn the symptoms of each disease.

INTERNAL PARASITES
(see p. 134)
- *Strongylus* (Large redworm)
- *Trichonema* (Small redworm)
- *Ascaris* (Whiteworm)
- *Anoplocephala* (Tapeworm)
- *Dictyocaulus* (Lungworm)
- *Oxyuris* (Pinworm)
- *Gasterophilus* (Bot)

JOINT DISORDERS
(see p. 124)
- Puffy joint
- Ringbone and sidebone
- Windgall
- Thoroughpin
- Spavin
- Curb
- Capped hock or elbow
- Patellar fixation
- Sesamoiditis
- Osteochondrosis (OCD)

FOOT DISORDERS
(see p. 122)
- Bruised sole
- Corn
- Laminitis
- Seedy toe
- Navicular disease
- Pedal ostitis
- Abscess in the foot
- Sand crack
- Thrush

SKIN DISORDERS
(see p. 130)
- Mud fever
- Cracked heels
- Rain scald
- Saddle sore and girth gall
- *Trichophyton* (Ringworm)
- *Hypoderma* (Warbles)
- Sweet itch
- *Haematopinus* and *Damalinia* (Lice)
- Mange

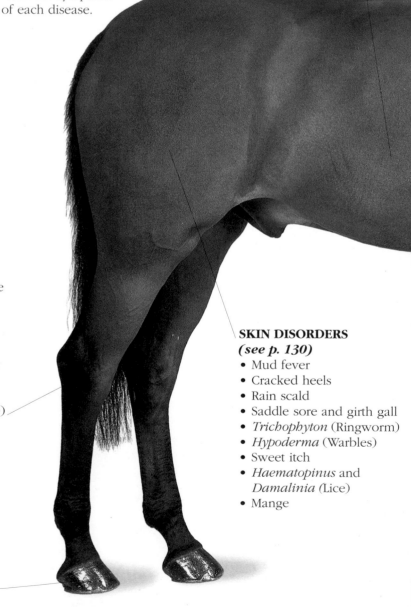

DIGESTIVE DISORDERS
(see p. 132)
- Colic
- Choke
- Diarrhoea
- Poisoning

EYE, NOSE, AND MOUTH DISORDERS
(see p. 128)
- Cataract
- Conjunctivitis
- Sinusitis
- Nose bleed
- Guttural pouch problems
- Dental problems
- Bit problems

RESPIRATORY DISORDERS
(see p. 138)
- Herpes virus infection
- Equine influenza
- Strangles
- Pneumonia
- *Dictyocaulus* (Lungworm)
- Laryngeal paralysis or hemiplegia (Roaring and whistling)
- Chronic obstructive pulmonary disease (COPD)

CIRCULATORY DISORDERS
(see p. 136)
- Anaemia
- Heart problems
- Dehydration
- Lymphangitis
- Azoturia
- Equine viral arteritis (EVA)
- African horse sickness (AHS)

LEG DISORDERS
(see p. 126)
- Sprained tendon
- Bowed tendon
- Broken knee
- Over reach
- Strike
- Tread
- Brushing
- Speedicut
- Splint
- Fracture
- Sore shin

WHEN TO CALL THE VET

When deciding whether or not to call the vet, bear these rules in mind:
- Never leave a horse in even slight pain for more than 24 hours without identifying the cause of the pain and dealing with it.
- Calling the vet is not an admission of failure. A vet is part of your team, and will in turn be relying on your first-aid treatment.
- Always base your decision on the horse's need rather than economics.

DIAGNOSING LAMENESS

When a horse is lame, it does not take its weight evenly on each leg as it moves. Lameness may be simple to cure, for example by removing a stone from the foot. It may be the result of an injury such as standing on a nail. It may be due to wear and tear on the leg joints. The cause may or may not be painful, but you should never work a lame horse except on the instructions of your vet. If the horse is badly lame call the vet immediately. If the lameness is only slight, stable the horse for 24–36 hours for rest; if it is still lame call the vet.

SIGNS OF LAMENESS

Holding a front foot off the ground is a warning sign; the foot is probably painful

Unusual behaviour
You may spot problems by seeing how the horse stands. If it is lame it may ease its weight off one leg, or shift uncomfortably when it is resting. It may rest a different leg than usual.

FINDING THE CAUSE OF LAMENESS

The use of hoof testers determines whether pressure on the hoof is painful

Veterinary examination
The vet may pinpoint the pain, and the cause of lameness, by using a nerve block – a local anaesthetic injected over a nerve, removing pain from the area temporarily. The sole of the foot may need paring, and the shoe may have to be removed.

A "big" leg
A swollen leg indicates a problem. Never ignore a swelling, even if the horse is not lame. Use a cold treatment (see p. 143) on the leg until you have a definite diagnosis.

Swelling may indicate a strained tendon

Normal leg

Swollen leg

IDENTIFYING THE LAME LEG

Trotting up for the vet

Lameness is most easily seen when a horse is trotted up in hand, because only at the trot do horses put an equal amount of weight on each leg. The horse must be trotted on a hard, level surface, so that you can hear whether it is sound or lame. In a sound horse the noise of all hooves will be identical; with a lame horse there will be a slightly louder and earlier noise when the corresponding good leg hits the ground. You will be asked to trot the horse up and down in a straight line while the vet watches the front of the horse and then its hindquarters.

Leave 30-45 cm (12–18 in) of loose rein to allow free movement of the head

The head nods as the horse puts weight on its good leg

Sound horse

Lame horse

Good leg

Lame leg

Lameness in a foreleg

When a sound horse trots, its head is held roughly level. When a horse that is lame on a foreleg trots, the head will nod when the good foreleg lands, because that leg is taking extra weight. Occasionally a horse will look slightly lame on a foreleg when the problem lies in the diagonal hind leg.

Sound hind legs

When a sound horse is trotted away from the viewer, its hips can be seen to stay level as its hindquarters move. As with sound forelegs, both feet in the pair will be lifted equally high off the ground, and will take an equal amount of weight when they land. The feet will hit the ground squarely.

Lameness in a hind leg

When a horse that is lame on a hind leg is trotted away from the viewer, the hips will be visibly uneven as the animal moves. The hindquarter on the good side will sink when the sound leg hits the ground, because that leg is taking extra weight. The hindquarters are not usually affected by lameness in a foreleg.

Lame leg

FOOT DISORDERS

Foot problems account for 90 per cent of all lameness. It is probably fair to say that most are due, at least in part, to a lack of care by the owner, such as leaving shoes on too long, not picking out the feet regularly, and overfeeding. Foot problems often affect more than one foot at a time, because all the feet undergo the same stresses or neglect. If a horse has a corn in one foot, it may well have a slight corn in one or more of its other feet. There is no point in treating the foot that appears to be lame, only for the horse to go lame on another foot shortly afterwards. It is better to check all the feet and learn the extent of the problem at the start, then treat it as a whole.

Paring the foot
In order to inspect the sole of the foot carefully, the vet will remove any flaking or discoloured horn with a drawing knife.

FOOT DISORDERS			
Symptoms	**Cause**	**Treatment**	**Prevention**
Bruised sole The horn around the white line may be discoloured. The horse is sensitive to pressure over the sole, and the lameness is worse on stony ground.	Treading on a hard object, or repeated pounding along the roads.	Rest the horse until the inflammation has subsided. It is a good idea to fit a protective pad that covers the sole.	Use a pad to protect the soles of horses with thin soles or flat feet.
Corn – bruising of the seat of corn, usually on a front foot Intermittent lameness, which usually worsens with exercise, especially on hard or uneven ground. When the seat of corn is pared, an area of discoloured horn is visible, often pink due to the presence of blood.	Poorly fitting shoes, or shoes being left on for too long before being replaced.	The farrier will remove discoloured horn and fit a special shoe that reduces percussion (repeated striking) on the area, because its ground surface is cut away over the corn.	Have your horse shod regularly by a good farrier.
 Horse with laminitis sinking back on its heels **Laminitis – inflammation of the sensitive laminae, usually in more than one foot** The horse tries to take weight off its toes, and sinks back on its heels. In acute cases it is unwilling to walk. The hooves will be warm.	Overeating or a toxic process causes the release into the bloodstream of chemicals that constrict small blood vessels such as those around the sensitive laminae of the feet. In some cases the laminae die, allowing the pedal bone to rotate and push through the sole of the foot.	Consult your vet and remove the underlying cause. Give the horse a complete rest; only in mild cases should you walk it out. Painkillers will help, and mild sedatives will lower blood pressure, and thus the pain. The feet should be trimmed to ensure a balanced foot (see p. 21), and special shoeing may be necessary.	Take great care with diet and looking after the feet, especially with ponies, which are particularly susceptible.

Symptoms	Cause	Treatment	Prevention
Seedy toe – infection in the foot The foot is painful when tapped on the area. Black pus, which may be dry and crumbly rather than liquid, travels up the foot at the toe through the white line.	A combination of poor-quality horn and a long toe, which pulls open the white line and allows the infection to enter.	All the infected horn must be removed.	Pick the feet out thoroughly to remove mud and manure, which can be the source of the infection.
Navicular disease – condition involving the navicular bone, the overlying deep flexor tendon, and the surrounding tissues in the heel, usually of both front feet Intermittent lameness in the early stages. The horse may potter when it trots, or stumble. It can be conclusively diagnosed by X-ray. Shadows in an X-ray of a diseased navicular bone	Probably wear and tear on the structures around the navicular bone, possibly caused by poor shoeing. This can be made worse by poor circulation.	Remedial shoeing is essential. Circulation can be helped by drugs that dilate the blood vessels. In some cases surgery may be necessary. An egg-bar shoe supporting the heel	Good shoeing can remove a possible cause of wear and tear.
Pedal ostitis – condition involving the navicular bone Similar to navicular disease.	Really a stage in the development of navicular disease, rather than a separate entity.	See navicular disease.	See navicular disease.
Abscess in the foot Dramatic lameness – the horse will not even put its foot to the ground.	Puncture of the sole of the foot, which allows infection into the sensitive tissues. The pus that forms has no means of escape, and the resulting pressure causes the pain.	The vet makes a hole in the foot large enough to allow the pus to drain out freely. Antibiotics may be needed, and the foot is usually poulticed to encourage drainage.	Check the feet regularly.
Sand crack – crack in the wall of the hoof A small, usually vertical crack, which will grow bigger if left. If it reaches the coronet it will prevent normal, uncracked horn from being made. The horse may be lame if the crack extends down to the sensitive tissues. Sand crack that has reached the coronet	Poor-quality horn that has not been sufficiently protected from stress by the shoe. Very dry conditions can make the horn liable to cracking.	The spread of the crack must be stopped as soon as possible. A horizontal groove above and at least as deep as the crack, or vertical grooves on either side of the crack, may stop it. In severe cases it may be necessary to cut away some horn and stabilise the crack with an acrylic artificial horn material.	Feed biotin and methionine supplements to ensure good-quality horn.
Thrush – infection of the frog The horn of the frog is black and smelly, and appears moist. The horse will be lame only in severe cases.	The horse being left to stand in a dirty, ill-drained stable or muddy conditions.	All infected horn must be removed, and it may help to apply an antibiotic spray or a diluted formalin solution to the remaining part of the frog.	Muck out the stable properly, so that the horse stands on clean material. Pick out the feet regularly.

JOINT DISORDERS

There are three important components of a joint from the disease point of view: the cartilage, the bone, and the joint fluid, which acts as both a lubricant for joint movement and the "food source" for cartilage. There are certain similarities between all conditions that affect joints. Until recently these problems were referred to as arthritis, but now we refer to them as degenerative joint disease or DJD. As a result of DJD, new bone can be formed and other areas of bone become less dense. These changes can be seen easily on X-ray. Damage to articular cartilage exposes raw bone underneath and is painful. Inflammation often results in the production of an increased amount of poor-quality joint fluid, which is why the affected joint appears swollen or puffy.

JOINT DISORDERS			
Symptoms	**Cause**	**Treatment**	**Prevention**
Puffy joint Swollen joint, but the horse is not lame and there is no pain.	A slight increase in the amount of joint fluid in response to long-term wear and tear.	No treatment is necessary in most cases. The swelling may decrease with rest.	Regular exercise, not extremes of inactivity and strenuous activity.
Ringbone and sidebone – joint disease, usually in older horses The horse is lame. X-rays show large amounts of new bone around the pastern. These may be big enough to feel. Ringbone is an enlargement of the pastern bones on or above the coronet; sidebone is a growth on the cartilage in the heel area.	Wear and tear from repeated concussion (vibration) of the pastern, e.g. during road work.	Usually there is no effective treatment, but painkillers may stop the lameness. If the new bone does not involve a joint (non-articular ringbone), it may settle down in time.	None.
Windgall – production of extra joint fluid Soft swelling at the back of the leg just above the fetlock, often worse after rest. The horse is not lame. A windgall	Wear and tear on the fetlock joint.	None necessary.	None possible, although good conformation – shoulders and pasterns that are not too upright – helps to avoid the problem.
Thoroughpin – production of extra joint fluid Soft swelling above the point of the hock between the bone and the tendon. A thoroughpin	Strain on the hock.	None necessary.	None, although good hock conformation helps to avoid the problem.

Symptoms	Cause	Treatment	Prevention
Spavin – bone enlargement The horse is lame on one or occasionally both hind legs. Sometimes a hard bony swelling can be seen low down on the inside of the hock.	A form of DJD involving the small bones of the hock joint.	Controlled exercise, with painkillers if necessary, may result in the painless fusion of bones. Surgical shoeing may help reduce lameness.	None, although good conformation helps to avoid the problem.
Curb – thickening of the ligament A firm swelling on the back of the leg at the bottom of the hock. The horse may or may not be lame as a result.	Excessive flexion of the hock joint, spraining the ligament linking some of the bones.	Rest the horse.	Good hocks are less at risk. Avoid working young horses in heavy going.
Capped hock or elbow – swelling on the joint Cold, painless swelling on the point of the hock or elbow. (Recent injuries are hot and soft.) The horse is not usually lame. A capped hock	May be caused by a blow, but often is the result of too little bedding, so that the horse injures the joint while lying down.	No treatment is necessary.	Use sufficient bedding. Fit sausage boots (see p. 173). Put travelling boots on for transport.
Patellar fixation or retention – locking of the stifle The hind leg is fixed rigidly behind the horse and the horse cannot bend it. This can occur during exercise or after another injury to the stifle joint. A rigid hind leg	The mechanism that enables the horse to lock its stifle and doze on its feet becomes activated by a shortening of one of the ligaments involved. This can be associated with the horse being in poor condition.	If the horse relaxes, it may be possible to relax the locking system by gently massaging the stifle joint. Surgery may be necessary to cut the shortened ligament and allow free movement again.	None.
Sesamoiditis – condition affecting the sesamoid bone Pain and swelling at the back of the fetlock joint.	Often the result of general wear and tear, but can occur due to a strain of the ligaments attached to the sesamoid bones.	Rest and treatment with anti-inflammatory drugs.	Avoid letting the foot develop a long-toe/ short-heel conformation.
Osteochondrosis (OCD) – bone disease of young horses The horse goes lame suddenly, often while standing in the stable overnight. It can affect a number of different joints, such as the stifle, hock, and fetlock. The capsule of the joint is swollen due to an increased amount of joint fluid.	The lameness is caused by the flaking away of a piece of cartilage from the joint, due to a weakness that developed during the first 6–12 months of a foal's life. The lameness does not occur until stress is put on the cartilage when the horse starts hard exercise.	Surgery to remove any cartilage and bone fragments from the joint is the only treatment.	None.

LEG DISORDERS

Enormous physical strains are placed on both the bones and the tendons of the horse's legs during exercise. For example, at certain stages of the gallop, the whole weight and momentum of the horse is taken by just one leg, so it is hardly surprising that problems arise. Leg injuries take a long time to heal, because it is not possible to prevent a horse from putting any weight on a leg for more than a very short time, so the affected leg can never be rested completely.

Laser treatment
The vet may use laser therapy to treat an injury. This treatment uses light energy to stimulate the horse's natural anti-inflammatory system.

LEG DISORDERS			
Symptoms	**Cause**	**Treatment**	**Prevention**
Sprained tendon, usually the long flexor tendon at the back of the cannon bone The tendon is thickened, and the tendon sheath that surrounds it becomes puffy and warm to the touch. The horse may be in great pain and does not want to put any weight on the leg. A horse with a severe sprain is said to be "broken down". Ultrasound scan of a sprained tendon *Area of ruptured tendon fibres is indicated by a black "hole", which will return to normal density as healing occurs*	Fast exercise, and sometimes a bandage being put on too tightly round the tendon.	Immediate cold treatment on the tendon. Arrange transport for the horse if the injury occurs away from home. Put support bandages on both the affected leg and the good leg, and give the horse complete stable rest in the early stages after the injury. Walk the horse out for 10–15 minutes twice a day, when the swelling has subsided (this may take 10–14 days). After a severe sprain, it may be 6–12 months before the horse can be ridden again. Laser or ultrasound therapy may help to reduce the inflammation, and anti-inflammatory drugs should be given.	Do not work a horse hard if it is unfit or tired. Never ignore any warning puffiness of the tendon. Feet with a long toe and short heels put extra strain on the tendons.
Bowed tendon – permanently swollen tendon A solid, firm swelling down the back of the flexor tendon. The horse is not lame.	This is the possible end result of a sprained tendon.	None. It is too late to treat the tendon. A bowed tendon is always weaker than a normal tendon, so care needs to be taken during exercise.	See sprained tendon.
Broken knee – injury to the knee This refers to an open wound on the front of the knee, rather than to a fracture.	The horse stumbling and falling down on the road.	Clean and dress the wound. If a lot of skin has been lost, healing will be slow and a scar may form.	Ride carefully on the road. Use knee boots (see p. 173).

Symptoms	Cause	Treatment	Prevention
Over reach – self-inflicted damage A horizontal cut or bruise on the heel or the back of the pastern of a foreleg. In very severe cases, the tendon may be cut.	A hind foot hitting a foreleg during exercise, possibly due to faulty action or conformation, or to poorly fitting shoes.	Clean and dress minor wounds. It may be possible to stitch a serious wound if it is fresh. Do not exercise the horse until the wound is healed. Prevent infection which will slow healing.	Trace and remove the cause if you can. Use over-reach boots (see p. 172) during exercise.
Strike – self-inflicted damage Similar to an over reach but higher up the leg, and it can cut the tendon.	See over reach.	See over reach.	As over reach but use tendon boots (see p. 172).
Tread – self-inflicted damage Wound in the coronet area.	The horse treading on itself or being trodden on by another horse.	See over reach.	Protect the leg for travelling. (See p. 173).
Brushing – self-inflicted damage Wound on the inside of the fetlock joint or the inside of the coronet.	A blow from the foot opposite the injured one.	See over reach.	As over reach but use brushing boots (see p. 172).
Speedicut – self-inflicted damage A wound on the inside of the knee or hock.	A blow from the toe of the opposite leg.	Seek veterinary advice. Do not ride without first seeking advice, because the horse could be unsafe.	Seek veterinary advice.
Splint – new bone formed on the wall of the cannon bone The horse may be lame with no obvious cause, but usually there is a hard swelling on the side of the cannon bone, which may be sore in the initial stages. *A splint*	Stress of repeated concussion (vibration) of the leg bones during exercise. The new bone growth forms to strengthen the wall of the cannon bone.	Cold treatments and anti-inflammatory drugs will help to reduce the inflammation. Most splints settle down with time and rest, and cause no further problems, although the hard swelling will always remain.	None.
Fracture – broken bone Extreme pain. The horse will usually be unable to use the affected leg. *A fractured leg*	Considerable force, but the stresses on a horse's legs during galloping can be so great that fractures occur with no obvious cause.	With modern technology it may be possible to repair a fracture of the hock, knee, and below. If the fracture is of a major bone higher than this, or if the bone has broken through the skin, the horse usually has to be put down.	None.
Sore shin – a condition of the cannon bone that affects young horses The horse is lame, and the front of one or both forecannons is painful to pressure. There may be heat and swelling.	Repeated pressure of work, which can overtax immature cannon bones.	Cold treatment and anti-inflammatory drugs combined with rest.	Do not overwork a young horse.

EYE, NOSE, & MOUTH DISORDERS

A horse in the wild would be severely handicapped by disorders affecting its senses. Domestic horses are not so vulnerable, because humans are able to compensate for impaired senses. For example, if we provide food for a horse it does not need to be able to distinguish between good and bad food or to seek it out. It is interesting that the muscles of the horse's eyelids are much more powerful than those of most other animals. They are able to close their eyes very quickly to protect them from injury, for example from branches as they gallop through trees. Unfortunately, this can make it very difficult to hold a horse's eye open to put in ointment or eye drops.

Inspecting an eye
The vet may need to look right into the horse's eye using an ophthalmoscope. This shines a light beam into the eye and contains a magnifying glass.

EYE, NOSE, AND MOUTH DISORDERS			
Symptoms	**Cause**	**Treatment**	**Prevention**
Cataract – degeneration of the lens of the eye The first indication may be that the horse fails to see people or danger approaching from one side. In certain lights the eye may appear cloudy or white. A cataract showing how it prevents light from passing through the lens, reflecting it instead	Most cataracts occur as horses get older. Some are hereditary and affect foals.	The lens can be removed surgically from the eye. This will return the horse's sight, although the horse might lose some of its ability to distinguish fine detail. No other treatment will help.	None.
Conjunctivitis – inflammation of the conjunctival membranes The membranes around the eye are red and swollen. There is usually a discharge from the eye; this may at first be watery, but later becomes more pus-like. An inflamed membrane – it can rapidly become infected	An irritant, such as a tiny piece of straw or some shampoo, getting into the eye. Infections can also cause conjunctivitis.	Remove anything in the eye. As long as the cornea has not been damaged, steroid eye ointments may be used to take away inflammation. Antibiotics will kill any infections.	None.

	Symptoms	Cause	Treatment	Prevention
Sinusitis – infection in the sinus The horse has a discharge from one nostril where pus is draining from the sinus into the nasal cavity. The sinus will sound solid when tapped with a finger, instead of hollow as it should.	This nasal discharge shows that it is the left side of the horse's skull that is affected	A tooth root abscess is the most common cause, because the roots of the molar teeth extend into the sinuses.	All the pus that has accumulated in the sinus must be drained out. Often, this is best done by removing the tooth whose root enters the sinus, to allow good drainage.	Regular dental checks help to avoid tooth root abscesses.
Nose bleed Blood, which in many cases comes from somewhere else in the respiratory system, drains from the horse's nose.	Blood draining from the left nostril	During strenuous exercise horses may bleed into their lungs, and the blood may become visible at the nose. A tumour in the nose can cause significant amounts of blood at the nostrils.	If blood loss has not been too great, clotting will occur if the horse is kept still, possibly by sedating it. The underlying cause then has to be dealt with.	Plenty of fresh air, and not too much strenuous exercise may reduce haemorrhage in the lungs.
Guttural pouch problems – problems with the large sac that opens off the passageway leading from the inner ear to the back of the throat Swelling behind the skin immediately below the ear, down the back of the jaw. There may be blood or pus in the sac, which will drain out via the nostrils.		Infections may have established themselves in the pouch. Also, the major arteries to the brain, which pass through the pouch, can become blocked.	Surgery may be necessary to prevent a possibly fatal haemorrhage.	None.
Dental problems The horse's performance may be reduced, and it may resent the pressure of the bit. It may quid (drop unchewed food out of its mouth while eating), or it may stop eating altogether.		An abscess will cause toothache. Sharp edges formed on the outside of the upper molars and the inside of the lower molars can cause ulcerations on the cheeks and tongue.	Any sharp edges must be rasped away. It may be necessary for the vet to remove a tooth.	Have your horse's teeth checked at least once a year.
Bit problems The horse may be unwilling to turn in one direction, or may toss its head in resentment when asked to do so. There may be bruising or ulceration of the gums immediately in front of the molar teeth.		A few horses have a very sensitive mouth, but nearly all problems are caused by a poorly fitting bridle.	Stop riding the horse for a while, then check the fit of the bridle. If possible, use a less severe bit.	Check the bit of a horse's bridle carefully every time you ride.

SKIN DISORDERS

It can be difficult to spot the onset of a skin problem, so skin disorders are often overlooked for too long. Some horses have a very thick coat, especially during winter. This can both hide diseases and provide good conditions for infections to multiply, so check a horse's coat carefully when you are grooming it. Use a grooming kit for one horse only. This prevents the spread of disease from one horse to another, and its importance cannot be stressed enough. The same applies to rugs and other clothes. Make sure, also, that the blades of clippers are sterile. It is a good idea to clip the hair around any skin problems. This will allow you to see what is happening, and treatment will be more effective. White-haired skin is more susceptible to many skin problems than pigmented skin.

SKIN DISORDERS

Symptoms	Cause	Treatment	Prevention
Mud fever Scabs on the skin, which are very sensitive. They are usually on the legs, especially on the pastern and fetlock, but can extend up to the belly. Sometimes the legs become swollen. Scabs on a leg (treated)	The infection *Dermatophilus congolensis* gains entry to the skin, because the skin is either softened by wet conditions or cracked by dry, dusty conditions. The scabs protect the bacteria underneath.	Remove the scabs to expose the infection to the air. Usually, the whole area must be clipped, because hair stabilises the scabs. Antiseptic shampoo may soften the scabs, and antibiotic cream will kill the infection. Antibiotic injections may be necessary.	Keep the pastern and fetlock areas clean and dry. If you have to wash mud off, dry the area thoroughly. When the infection has cleared, apply petroleum jelly to protect the skin in the wet.
Cracked heels – a form of mud fever Horizontal oozing wounds on the back of the pasterns. Scabs may develop. Horses with white socks are particularly susceptible.	Infection gaining entry to the skin. See mud fever.	See mud fever.	See mud fever.
Rain scald – an infection similar to mud fever Tufts of hair held together by small scabs all over the body. These often appear after rain or damp conditions. Scab (treated)	Infection with *Dermatophilus*, which spreads rapidly over the wet skin.	As for mud fever, although clipping may not be possible.	Provide the horse with shelter from the rain.
Saddle sore and girth gall – area of rubbed skin Raised inflamed area of skin in the saddle and girth area. It may become raw. A severe saddle sore with hair clipped away	Poorly fitting tack, or a foreign body trapped under the saddle, or girth rubbing the skin.	Remove the cause and do not ride the horse again until the skin has healed.	Ensure that the saddle and girth are clean and fit properly. A gel pad under the saddle (see p. 155) will distribute pressure.

	Symptoms	Cause	Treatment	Prevention
Trichophyton (Ringworm) – a fungal infection	Typically round areas of hair loss or slight crusting anywhere on the body. The skin and hair may just look tatty rather than showing such areas. *Ringworm crusting around an eye*	A fungus weakens the base of the hairs, which break off. The infection can be passed on by grooming kit and tack, or from the stable or wood surfaces. It is often carried by cattle.	Special antibiotics will kill the fungus, although it will be some time before the hair regrows. In time, the horse usually becomes immune to the infection.	The fungal spores live for many months. Treat affected surfaces with an antibiotic before using them. Keep the horse away from infected cattle.
Hypoderma (Warbles) – the larvae of warble flies	A raised area on the horse's back near its backbone, occurring during the winter. In the spring a hole may appear in the centre.	The warble fly lays its eggs on the horse's legs. The larvae burrow into the skin and make their way to the horse's back, where they develop and form swellings. In the spring, adult flies may emerge, although some stay there for a considerable time.	Ivermectin will kill the warble larvae, but it may be necessary to remove the hard lump surgically.	None.
Sweet itch – an allergy to midges	Lost hair and raw and oozing skin at the base of the mane and tail during the summer. *Short, broken hairs, which are the result of sweet itch*	The horse rubs its mane and tail because of an allergy to the saliva of small midges that bite the affected areas.	There is no cure for the allergy. Benzyl benzoate lotion will soothe the rubbed areas and kill midges. Calamine lotion is also soothing.	Stable the horse during the evening and morning, when the midges are active. Use fly-repellent washes on the horse's skin and in the stable.
Haematopinus and _Damalinia_ (Lice) – parasitic insects Large areas of bald skin in winter. *Hair loss due entirely to rubbing*	The horse rubs itself to relieve the irritation of active lice that bite or suck the skin. *A louse – well designed for biting and sucking*	Repeated doses of ivermectin will kill lice.	A horse should be treated if it comes into contact with lice, whether it is showing symptoms or not.	
Mange – inflammation caused by tiny mites (_Psoroptes_ and _Chorioptes_) The affected areas, usually the lower legs, are intensely irritated. The horse stamps its feet and tries to rub them.	The mites bite. There are several families of mange mites. _Chorioptes_ and _Psoroptes_ are the most common.	When available, benzene hexachloride (BHC) shampoos are effective.	See lice.	

DIGESTIVE DISORDERS

There are several inherent weaknesses in the horse's digestive system (see p. 27). This means that the horse is prone to digestive disorders, the main one being colic. There are three types of colic: impaction, spasmodic colic, and physical displacement. Impaction is when there is no movement of material along a portion of the horse's bowel. The horse may still pass droppings initially, as it empties out the bowel contents below the impaction. The pain is low-level, constant discomfort, so the horse may lie on its side, unwilling to move. Impactions often follow a change of diet, when a new type of fibre has not been digested. Sometimes impactions are associated with tapeworm infestations. In spasmodic colic, as its name implies, the pain comes and goes. The pain is usually associated with excess bowel activity. It may follow a disturbance of some sort that upsets the horse temporarily. A physical displacement is often referred to as a twisted gut. A section of the digestive tract becomes completely displaced, with the result that pressure from the organs interferes with the blood supply to the affected area. Straightforward twisting around of a section of the bowel is relatively uncommon. The pain can be severe, and the horse becomes very shocked. Surgery may be the only form of successful treatment. Rolling may be a symptom of a physical displacement, but it does not cause a displacement.

DIGESTIVE DISORDERS

Symptoms	Cause	Treatment	Prevention
Colic – abdominal pain It is important that you know how to recognize colic in the early stages. The horse usually stops eating and may start to look round at its belly. Areas of patchy swelling appear over its body. It may then start stamping at the ground with its front feet or kicking at its belly with its hind feet. As the pain becomes more intense, the horse will lie down. In acute pain it will roll over repeatedly, oblivious to anything or anybody. Its pulse may increase to 60 or 80 beats per minute.	Many different causes, affecting quite different parts of the horse's digestive tract, will result in the same colic symptoms.	Call the vet at once. Stable the horse, if possible with a thick bed in case it starts to roll. Encourage it to eat a warm bran mash. Do not walk the horse endlessly round and round; this will not affect the course of the colic, but will tire the horse and may mean that it rolls in an unsuitable place. Do not try to drench (give liquid medicine to) the horse. In its pain it may not swallow, and the liquid may go into its lungs.	Feed your horse regular amounts of food at regular intervals. Follow a suitable feeding regime (see p. 108) and make any diet change gradually, over 7–10 days. Follow a comprehensive worming programme (see p. 134). Have your horse's teeth checked regularly.

A horse pawing the ground – a symptom of colic

Operating to relieve colic

Symptoms	Cause	Treatment	Prevention
Choke – food stuck in the gullet The horse is very distressed. Copious amounts of frothy saliva come down its nostrils and drool out of its mouth. The horse cannot eat or drink, and a swelling may be visible on the left side of its neck. Saliva coming from the nostrils and mouth, caused by choke	Large pieces of apple or root vegetable such as carrot are common things to get stuck. Unsoaked sugar beet can also get stuck, because it swells up quickly on contact with water. The saliva produced cannot drain down past the obstruction, and so overflows.	Gentle massage of any swelling may encourage the obstruction to pass on. The vet may need to use a stomach tube to remove the saliva, which otherwise might trickle down the horse's windpipe.	Take care to cut up food properly (see p. 111).
Diarrhoea Loose droppings, varying from cow-pat consistency to brown water. The horse will start to dehydrate if diarrhoea continues for more than an hour or two. If it continues for days, the horse will lose body proteins faster than it can take them in, and will start to lose weight. A horse that has lost weight due to diarrhoea	There are many causes. Bacteria such as salmonella, heavy worm infestations, and lush spring grass can all cause diarrhoea. Diseases that damage the intestinal wall may stop the horse absorbing water from the bowel and result in diarrhoea. Stress or excitement may also lead to this problem.	The cause should be diagnosed and treated accordingly. Special electrolyte (salt) mixtures will stop the horse from dehydrating. Codeine can be useful in stopping the diarrhoea	Worm the horse regularly and avoid subjecting it to severe stress.
Poisoning Many poisons start by causing mild constipation, which is then followed by diarrhoea. In cases of severe poisoning, the horse can become extremely distressed.	The horse may have eaten a poisonous plant (see p. 84) or ingested one of many toxic chemicals with its grass. These range from lead in a discarded battery to a seed dressing applied to corn.	Give the horse a bran mash or liquid paraffin to speed up the passage of the poison through the system. The symptoms have to be treated rather than the poison, as there are few specific antidotes.	Check your field regularly and remove all poisonous plants and dumped rubbish. Keep chemicals away from the stableyard.

INTERNAL PARASITES

The basic relationship between parasitic worms and horses is that the adult worm lives in the horse's bowel, surrounded by the food that passes through the horse's digestive tract. Often, the worm attaches itself to the bowel wall to stop itself from being carried right through the horse with food and water. It is not in the parasite's interests to kill the horse because, if it does, the worms in that horse will die too. In the wild, where horses roam over a wide area, they rarely develop a worm burden severe enough to be fatal. When they are restricted to grazing a small area continuously, as are domestic horses in a field, the number of worms they take in can be enormous and possibly lethal.

DEVELOPMENT OF THE WORM

Worms on pasture
A pasture with worm eggs and larvae is like a time bomb, which will explode when horses graze there. There are no chemicals that kill worm eggs. Drying out and extremes of temperature will kill them in time, but this can take two or three years. When the eggs hatch, the larvae climb to the top of grass stalks. Topping (cutting the grass) will remove these larvae; dividing the grazing up and using each area in turn will allow time for larvae to die in between grazing periods. The larvae develop in the horse, and cause more damage than adult worms. You must therefore worm the horse regularly, not just when you know you have a problem.

Life-cycle of the worm

The larvae moult several times inside the horse, shedding their skin and getting bigger and bigger until the adult worms develop

The larvae are eaten with the grass by a horse

The adult worms release eggs, which eventually pass out with the horse's droppings

The droppings break down, and the worm larvae hatch and climb up the grass stalks

WORMING PROGRAMMES

There are three anthelmintics, or worming drugs, that are active against a reasonably wide range of worms: ivermectin, pyrantel, and the benzimidazoles (all of whose chemical names end in "-ndazole"). It is not possible to control all worms with just one wormer; you must target-worm for the exceptions, and then have one drug for routine use throughout the year. Change the type of wormer every one or two years. You should not change it every time you dose, as this will make it easier for the worms to become resistant to the wormers. There are no resistance problems with ivermectin and pyrantel, but in some parts of the world there is resistance to the benzimidazole wormers. To prevent a significant number of worm eggs from being released on your pasture you should worm every four weeks with a benzimidazole wormer, every six weeks with pyrantel, or every eight weeks with ivermectin.

HOW WORMS AFFECT THE HORSE

Does your horse have worms?

You will not be able to tell if your horse has worms by just looking at it. Most worms cause a loss of condition, but there are other factors that make a horse thin. A large number of adult worms or larvae is usually needed to cause weight loss, anaemia, or general poor condition. Worms can be associated with colic (see p. 132). A horse that has repeated colic attacks, or colic where no other cause is diagnosed, should be wormed. Different tests are needed to identify which worms are present. The identification and quantity of *Strongylus*, *Ascaris*, *Trichonema*, and *Oxyuris* worms can usually be determined by having some of the horse's dung tested for eggs.

THE MAIN WORMS THAT AFFECT HORSES	
Worm	**Target control**
Strongylus (Large redworm) The larvae spend several months in the blood vessels that supply the bowel. They obstruct the blood flow, and so can be dangerous. They emerge in the bowel and can then cause diarrhoea. Because they are larvae and not adult worms, their presence will not be detected by a worm egg count.	Use ivermectin, because it kills the larvae in the blood vessels as well as the adults.
Trichonema (Small redworm) Larvae can lie dormant in cysts in the intestinal wall, before a large number suddenly emerge.	Large or repeated doses of fenbendazole may kill dormant larvae. The best control is to prevent the build-up of larvae.
Ascaris (Whiteworm) These pass through the lungs during development, causing coughing and a nasal discharge in young horses. Horses over a year old seem to develop an immunity against them.	Treat young horses from 6 weeks old with ivermectin, pyrantel, or a benzimidazole wormer.
Anoplocephala (Tapeworm) These flatworms live in the area around the junction between the small intestine and the caecum. They can cause impactions to form at this junction, which can lead to colic. They need an intermediate host – a mite found on grass – to complete their life-cycle.	A double dose of pyrantel in the early autumn every 1–2 years.
Dictyocaulus (Lungworm) As their name suggests, they live in the lungs, and cause the horse to cough. The immature larvae are carried up the trachea (windpipe) and then swallowed. The full life-cycle occurs in donkeys. In horses, it usually stops when the larvae reach the lungs.	Use ivermectin, especially where horses and donkeys are grazed together.
Oxyuris (Pinworm) The adult worms live just inside the rectum. Larvae develop in eggs, then drop to the ground.	Routine worming with most modern wormers will control the worms.
Gasterophilus (Bot) Strictly speaking, these are not worms. The bot fly lays eggs on the horse's skin, which are licked up and pass to the stomach where the larvae develop. The adult fly emerges only after the larvae have been passed in the droppings.	Give ivermectin in winter.

CIRCULATORY DISORDERS

The state of a horse's blood gives a good indication of the animal's health. When a blood sample is taken, the vet examines the red and white blood cells and the blood fluid, or plasma. The number of red cells, and the amount of haemoglobin they contain, indicate whether or not a horse has anaemia. White blood cells are affected by infections: bacterial infections cause an increased number of a cell called a neutrophil; parasitic infections increase the numbers of a cell called an eosinophil. Plasma contains substances that have escaped from cells in the internal organs. Background low levels of the substances are present all the time, but if an organ is diseased the plasma levels will be affected. For example, liver disease will result in a raised level of a substance called gamma glutamyltransferase. Modern technology allows vets to measure about 20 of these different characteristics of blood in their own surgery.

Taking blood
The vet may take a blood sample to analyse the red and white cells. The sample must be taken from a horse completely at rest.

CIRCULATORY DISORDERS			
Symptoms	**Cause**	**Treatment**	**Prevention**
Anaemia – reduced number of red blood cells in the blood or decreased haemoglobin in the cells The horse is dull and lethargic. The pink membranes around the eyes and mouth become paler. Anaemia will have become severe before symptoms are noted.	A deficiency of folic acid can lead to a decrease in the manufacture of red blood cells. Anaemia is caused by chronic internal bleeding or severe bloodsucking by worms. Contrary to popular opinion, it is hardly ever due to an iron or vitamin B$_{12}$ deficiency.	A folic acid supplement will always be worthwhile. Any other cause should be treated accordingly. Recovery will take some time, because it takes at least a month for the body to replace red blood cells.	Worm the horse regularly. Give access to fresh grass, which provides folic acid.
Heart problems In severe cases, the horse may have oedema (filling) of the legs or underneath the belly. The existence of heart murmurs or abnormal heart beats does not mean that the horse will suddenly collapse.	There is no one cause. An electrocardiograph may indicate why the horse's heart rhythms have been affected.	There is little precise treatment.	None.

Symptoms	Cause	Treatment	Prevention
Dehydration – lack of water in the body The horse is weak and lethargic. It might collapse or appear dazed. If you pull up a fold of skin on the neck and then let it go, it will remain in place rather than go back to normal instantly.	The horse not drinking, or losing too much water – for instance through diarrhoea. Dehydration may also be due to loss of electrolytes (salts) when the horse sweats.	An immediate supply of electrolyte supplement. In severe cases, an intravenous transfusion may be necessary.	Give the horse access to fresh water at all times. Make sure that it drinks during long rides.
Lymphangitis – damage to the lymphatics (tubes that drain the tissue fluid away) One or both hind legs are swollen due to the presence of tissue fluid. If the leg becomes greatly swollen, fluid may start to ooze through the skin. Swollen hind leg due to lymphangitis	Imbalance between food and exercise. It used to be called Monday morning disease because it used to occur in cart-horses after their rest day. (Azoturia [see below] is also sometimes called Monday morning disease for the same reason.)	Hot fomentations on the groin area may help circulation. A diuretic drug may remove some of the fluid.	Reduce food on rest days.
Azoturia – damage to the muscles by high levels of lactic acid The horse is suddenly very stiff and unwilling to move. It may pass dark red urine. The muscles of the back and hindquarters may be hard and swollen.	Too much food on a rest day, causing a high level of lactic acid to be formed by the muscles during the next period of exercise. The acid cannot be removed effectively by the circulation, and damages the muscles.	Do not exercise the horse any further. Seek veterinary help. Keep the muscles warm with rugs to help the circulation.	Do not overfeed the horse for the work it is doing (see p. 107), as this leads to more lactic acid being formed.
Equine viral arteritis (EVA) – infectious disease that damages the tiny arteries Flu-like symptoms.	A virus.	No specific treatment.	Vaccination is possible.
African horse sickness (AHS) Large raised areas of swelling on the body. It is usually fatal, because the swellings press on the airways, preventing the horse from breathing.	A virus carried by a midge. It only occurs in countries warm enough to allow the midge to survive through the winter.	No treatment. Affected horses are usually put down to prevent them from infecting other horses.	Vaccination is possible.

RESPIRATORY DISORDERS

One of the main symptoms of a respiratory problem is a cough. Coughing is a protective mechanism to keep the airways free of mucus. The vet should concentrate on removing the cause rather than suppressing the cough itself. All horses cough occasionally, but you should note if the horse coughs more than three or four times consecutively. A cough will spread infection by propelling tiny droplets of water and bacteria into the air. Not all coughs are infectious, though, so a coughing horse does not necessarily pose a threat to other horses.

Listening to the lungs

The vet listens with a stethoscope to the sounds made by air entering and leaving the lungs. Abnormalities in the lungs can be detected this way.

RESPIRATORY DISORDERS

Symptoms	Cause	Treatment	Prevention
Herpes virus infection A nasal discharge and a cough. Occasionally, when more serious, the herpes virus can cause abortion or paralysis.	A virus.	Drugs to keep the airways open and free from mucus.	Vaccination may be possible.
Equine influenza – flu The horse has a cough, runny eyes, and a runny nose. It may have a high temperature. Chronic lung or heart problems may follow after the flu has been overcome. In foals, equine influenza can be fatal. *A runny nose*	One of two main families of virus.	There is no specific treatment. Drugs to keep the airways open and to kill secondary infections are usually given.	Vaccination.
Strangles – a contagious throat infection Large abscesses under the jaw and around the throat. The horse has a high temperature. In time, the abscesses burst, releasing foul-smelling pus. If they burst internally, the horse will have a pus-filled nasal discharge. *A swollen gland due to an abscess*	A bacterial infection.	Antibiotics, given after the abscesses have burst, will kill the infection.	A vaccine is available in some countries.

Symptoms	Cause	Treatment	Prevention
Pneumonia – infection in the lungs The horse has difficulty in breathing and may have an increased respiratory rate (see p. 43). It may cough.	A virus or bacteria that damages the lung tissues. Foals can suffer from a particularly serious form of pneumonia.	Bacterial pneumonias may respond to antibiotics; viral pneumonias never will. There are drugs available that help to remove mucus from the lungs and open the airways.	Make sure that the stable is well ventilated (see p. 97).
***Dictyocaulus* (Lungworm) (see p. 135)** A persistent cough that starts while the horse is at grass during the summer.	See p. 135.	See p. 135.	See p. 135.
Laryngeal paralysis or hemiplegia (Roaring and whistling) – paralysis of a vocal cord Most of the time the horse shows no sign of illness at all. Only during very strenuous exercise may a roaring sound be heard as the horse breathes in. The horse's athletic performance is reduced.	The horse is usually born with this condition. One of the vocal cords, usually the left, is paralysed either wholly or partially. It cannot be pulled out of the way to allow more air to get into the trachea. *Cartilage* *Paralysed vocal cord* *Trachea* *Epiglotis* Abnormal trachea	If performance is affected then surgery will be required to pull the vocal cord out of the way permanently. *Corrected vocal cord* Trachea after surgery	None.
Chronic obstructive pulmonary disease (COPD) – a restriction of small airways in the lungs The horse has to make a conscious effort to empty its lungs completely. It may have a cough and a nasal discharge. Athletic performance will be reduced. A "heave" line from the stifle along the belly may be visible, where increased muscle effort has been needed to push air out of the lungs.	An allergy to fungal spores on hay and straw. Occasionally other particles, such as pollen, can trigger the condition.	Turn the horse out, or make sure it does not come into contact with hay or straw. There are drugs that open up the constricted airways, and nebulizers for drugs that protect the lungs of affected horses. Breathing via a nebulizer	Use alternative spore-free bedding (see p. 99) and feed vacuum-packed grass rather than hay (see p. 113).

WHEN TO CALL THE VET

Use your common sense when assessing whether to call the vet. You should know your horse's habits, past problems, and normal lumps. If you are not sure if your horse has a serious problem or not, call the vet to dicuss it. Never leave a horse with an unexplained condition for more than 24 hours.

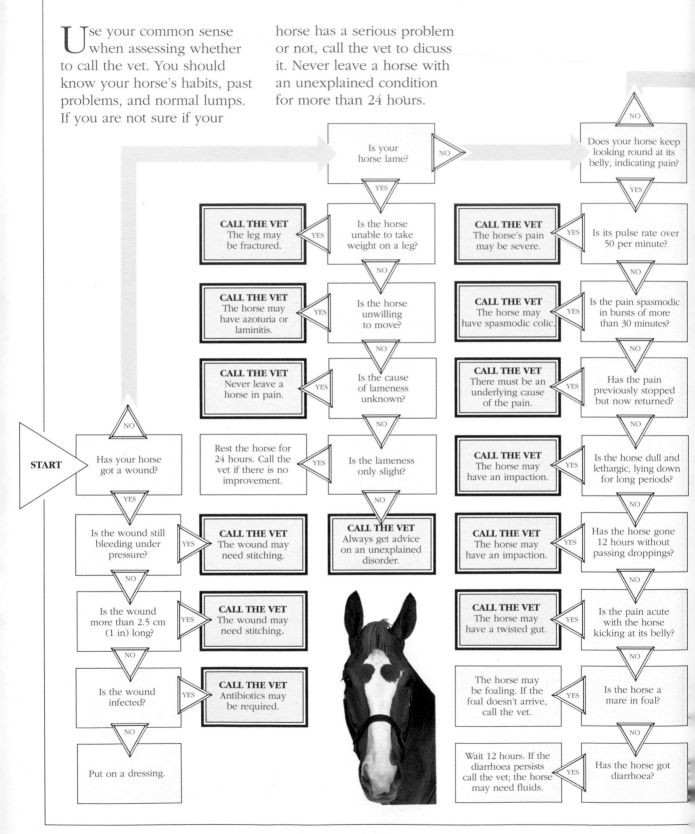

Is your horse lame?

NO →

Does your horse keep looking round at its belly, indicating pain?

NO

YES

CALL THE VET The leg may be fractured. ← YES — **Is the horse unable to take weight on a leg?**

CALL THE VET The horse's pain may be severe. ← YES — **Is its pulse rate over 50 per minute?**

NO

CALL THE VET The horse may have azoturia or laminitis. ← YES — **Is the horse unwilling to move?**

CALL THE VET The horse may have spasmodic colic. ← YES — **Is the pain spasmodic in bursts of more than 30 minutes?**

NO

CALL THE VET Never leave a horse in pain. ← YES — **Is the cause of lameness unknown?**

CALL THE VET There must be an underlying cause of the pain. ← YES — **Has the pain previously stopped but now returned?**

NO

START →

Has your horse got a wound?

NO

Rest the horse for 24 hours. Call the vet if there is no improvement. ← YES — **Is the lameness only slight?**

CALL THE VET The horse may have an impaction. ← YES — **Is the horse dull and lethargic, lying down for long periods?**

NO

YES

Is the wound still bleeding under pressure? — YES → **CALL THE VET** The wound may need stitching.

CALL THE VET Always get advice on an unexplained disorder.

CALL THE VET The horse may have an impaction. ← YES — **Has the horse gone 12 hours without passing droppings?**

NO

Is the wound more than 2.5 cm (1 in) long? — YES → **CALL THE VET** The wound may need stitching.

CALL THE VET The horse may have a twisted gut. ← YES — **Is the pain acute with the horse kicking at its belly?**

NO

Is the wound infected? — YES → **CALL THE VET** Antibiotics may be required.

The horse may be foaling. If the foal doesn't arrive, call the vet. ← YES — **Is the horse a mare in foal?**

NO

Put on a dressing.

Wait 12 hours. If the diarrhoea persists call the vet; the horse may need fluids. ← YES — **Has the horse got diarrhoea?**

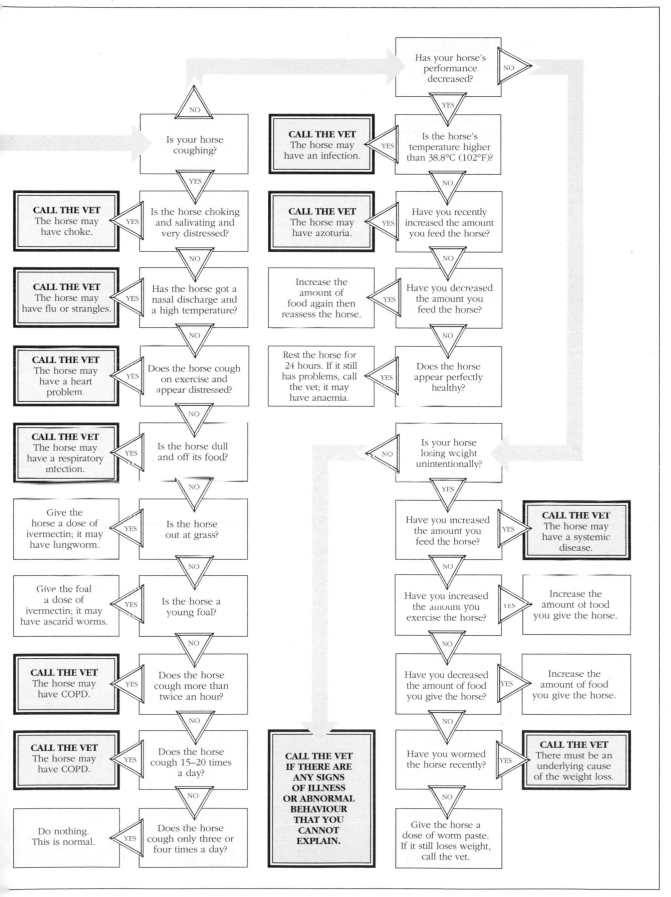

Has your horse's performance decreased?

NO

Is your horse coughing?

CALL THE VET The horse may have an infection.

YES

Is the horse's temperature higher than 38.8°C (102°F)?

NO

YES

CALL THE VET The horse may have choke.

YES

Is the horse choking and salivating and very distressed?

CALL THE VET The horse may have azoturia.

YES

Have you recently increased the amount you feed the horse?

NO

NO

CALL THE VET The horse may have flu or strangles.

YES

Has the horse got a nasal discharge and a high temperature?

Increase the amount of food again then reassess the horse.

YES

Have you decreased the amount you feed the horse?

NO

NO

CALL THE VET The horse may have a heart problem.

YES

Does the horse cough on exercise and appear distressed?

Rest the horse for 24 hours. If it still has problems, call the vet; it may have anaemia.

YES

Does the horse appear perfectly healthy?

NO

CALL THE VET The horse may have a respiratory infection.

YES

Is the horse dull and off its food?

NO

Is your horse losing weight unintentionally?

NO

YES

Give the horse a dose of ivermectin; it may have lungworm.

YES

Is the horse out at grass?

Have you increased the amount you feed the horse?

YES

CALL THE VET The horse may have a systemic disease.

NO

NO

Give the foal a dose of ivermectin; it may have ascarid worms.

YES

Is the horse a young foal?

Have you increased the amount you exercise the horse?

YES

Increase the amount of food you give the horse.

NO

NO

CALL THE VET The horse may have COPD.

YES

Does the horse cough more than twice an hour?

Have you decreased the amount of food you give the horse?

YES

Increase the amount of food you give the horse.

NO

NO

CALL THE VET The horse may have COPD.

YES

Does the horse cough 15–20 times a day?

CALL THE VET IF THERE ARE ANY SIGNS OF ILLNESS OR ABNORMAL BEHAVIOUR THAT YOU CANNOT EXPLAIN.

Have you wormed the horse recently?

YES

CALL THE VET There must be an underlying cause of the weight loss.

NO

NO

Do nothing. This is normal.

YES

Does the horse cough only three or four times a day?

Give the horse a dose of worm paste. If it still loses weight, call the vet.

FIRST-AID EQUIPMENT

You never know where or when an injury may be sustained, so you do not know where or when you will need a first-aid kit. Certainly you must have one at the stables. When you travel to shows you need one in the horsebox or trailer, and if you go out on long hacks you should also take a very simple kit with you. The stable kit, and any more basic first-aid kit, should be kept in a dry, clean place such as the tack room, where everyone can find it easily. Remember to keep this equipment well out of the way of small children. All first-aid kits should be checked regularly and, if necessary, re-stocked, so that dressings and other items are always there when needed.

Saddle bag
When you go out riding, take a small first-aid kit in a saddle bag. You can buy a ready-made kit, or make up your own to include enough to deal with a wound: a cleaning agent, a non-stick dressing, padding, and a bandage. You will not have room for more.

ANTISEPTICS

Liquids
The best antiseptic is chlorhexidine. A concentrated liquid antiseptic must be diluted with clean water before use. This is fine for a stable kit, but in a saddle kit it must be ready for use.

Aerosol sprays
An antiseptic in a spray is easier than liquid to apply directly to small wounds to prevent infection. The noise may startle a horse, but it need be applied only lightly.

BANDAGES

Ventilated elastic adhesive bandage
Usually you should not use these directly on the skin, but in a few cases this is the only way to hold a dressing. A warm bandage sticks better than a cold one.

Zip-up lycra bandage
Bandaging a knee or hock takes practice. There are specially designed zip-up lycra bandages that are easier to put on. They are shaped for particular joints, and come in different sizes.

Crepe bandage
This has "give" in it, making it cling to the leg, but with use it will lose this. It is secured by splitting the end and tying it round the leg, or with a safety pin and a stable bandage on top.

Self-adhesive bandage
Cohesive bandages stick only to themselves, and mould to the shape of the leg. They will not stretch or contract if swelling increases or goes down, so they may have to be re-applied if this happens.

DRESSING ITEMS

Scissors
Every first-aid kit needs a pair of good scissors for jobs like cutting dressings to shape and trimming hair. Scissors should have sharp blades with rounded ends. Blunt scissors must be replaced.

Gamgee
This material consists of cotton wool between layers of gauze. It does not shed fibres like plain cotton wool. It can be wrapped around a leg, but does not shape to the leg without being trimmed.

All-purpose dressing
Prepared dry poultice dressings are soaked in warm water before use. Never leave a poultice on for more than 48 hours, or the skin at the wound edges will die. The plastic layer goes on the outside.

Gauze
Impregnated gauze dressings are convenient for stopping bandages and other coverings from sticking to wounds. The dressings contain either petroleum jelly or, more usefully, an antibiotic gel.

Perforated plastic film
Plastic film also does not stick to wounds. The perforations in the plastic film allow fluid from the wound to pass through it, and the fluid is then absorbed by a lint pad on the outside of the dressing.

Hydrophilic polyurethane
This type of dressing provides padding as well as ensuring good conditions for healing. The special foam draws fluid away from the wound, and can absorb up to 10 times its own weight.

COLD TREATMENTS

Freeze pack
Specially designed freeze packs can be bought and kept in a freezer until needed. The "bubbles" of liquid in this pack give it flexibility, and allow it to mould to the horse's leg even when the pack has just come out of the freezer.

Cold pack
A gel that never quite freezes solid is contained inside this type of pack. The pack is kept in the freezer until needed and then stays cold for a considerable length of time. It is rather heavy, so special straps are provided to hold the pack in place.

Hosing boot
The boot allows a continuous flow of cold water to be applied to a horse's cannon. It is directly attached to a flexible hosepipe, and strapped to a horse's leg like an ordinary tendon boot (see p. 172). After use, it must be dried thoroughly before storage.

FIRST AID

First aid is not an alternative to calling the vet. As its name implies, it is what you do first of all when you find a wound or other problem. Whether you then need to call a vet may depend on the results of your efforts. There are situations when you should always seek veterinary help (see p. 140). The basis of first aid is calmness. Don't let yourself panic or rush things. If you do, the dressings will slip or the bandages will unroll, and you will become frustrated. Although you know that you are trying to help the horse, the horse does not; an injured horse is entitled to be scared and uncooperative. Try to pass on some of your confidence to the horse.

USING A SPRAY

A small wound on the neck is suitable for a light application of antibiotic spray

Antibiotic spray
Hold the can upright 30–48 cm (12–19 in) from the skin and spray briefly. Some horses dislike the noise, so spray in the air first, to assess the horse's reaction. It will probably get used to it. Cotton wool plugs in the ears may help if there is a problem.

CLEANING A WOUND

When and how to do it
Don't clean a wound unless you are sure you will do more good than harm. Wash your hands first, and make sure that water and swabs are clean. It is better to use a sterile, dry swab than risk introducing infection with non-sterile water. Never use dirty water from a bucket. Don't keep washing a wound just because it bleeds – washing will disturb the necessary formation of clots. Finally, don't be mesmerized by a little blood and fail to spot a more serious problem.

1 Start cleaning at the centre of a wound, no matter what size it is. Use clean cotton wool with a weak saline or antiseptic solution.

2 Work outwards, so that you do not bring dirt into the wound from the surrounding skin. Do not push dirt under any skin flaps.

3 Finally, clean the skin surrounding the wound. Never go back to the wound with the same swab, even if the wound is still bleeding.

DRESSING A WOUND ON A LEG

Use of dressings
The main reason for dressing a wound is to use pressure to stop bleeding. In some cases, this is more important than washing the wound. Take care to apply even pressure. If tight pressure is needed, it must be released every 30 minutes to let the blood flow to the rest of the area. Most wounds hurt much less when dressed.

1 Apply a non-stick dressing first. This will not disturb the blood clot when you change it.

2 Wrap padding around the leg. Don't worry if the wound is bleeding – it can take up to 30 minutes to stop.

3 Bandage over the padding. Start at the top, to secure the dressing, then move down to the wound area.

4 Use all the bandage, leaving an edge of padding at top and bottom. Take time to do it well.

APPLYING A FOMENTATION

A hot fomentation
This involves the application of warmth to an injured area to reduce pain or swelling. It is useful for areas on which a poultice cannot be strapped – for example, the stifle. Soak a cloth in warm water. (If it is too hot for you, then it is too hot to go on the horse.) Squeeze out some of the water, then hold the cloth in position on the injured area. When it loses heat, replace it with another one, continuing for at least 15–20 minutes. This is tiring, but unless you apply a hot fomentation for this length of time, it is not worth doing.

Apply gentle pressure and be ready for any reaction from the horse

BANDAGING A KNEE

ZIP-UP BANDAGE

A commercial zip-up bandage is particularly useful if a dressing needs to be changed often, because it is easy to put on and take off. Wrap the bandage around the knee, and secure it in position with the velcro fastenings. Then do up the zip, being careful not to catch any hairs or dressing in the teeth.

Applying a figure-of-eight bandage
A horse's knees are vulnerable to injury, but prompt first aid can speed up healing tremendously. A figure-of-eight bandage is necessary to hold a dressing in place on the moving joint.

1 Dress the wound then wrap padding around the leg. Anchor the padding at the top with two or three turns of bandage. Bring the bandage diagonally down across the knee, and make a complete turn around the leg at the bottom of the padding.

Hold the padding in place as you bandage

Keep the padding flat underneath the bandage

2 Take the bandage diagonally up across the knee again to produce a cross of bandage on the front of the knee. This applies pressure to a wound on the knee and will not be disturbed when the horse moves its leg.

3 Bandage around the leg at the top and then work downwards in the normal way. Overlap at least half of the previous layer of bandage with each new turn until you reach the bottom of the padding. If the bandage is long enough, make a second figure of eight before finishing off.

4 The finished bandage looks like an ordinary one because the figure of eight is covered. When you bandage, make sure that you keep the same tension throughout and that each layer lies flat.

BANDAGING A HOCK

Covering the hock joint

The hock is awkward to bandage in the ordinary way, because the layers of bandage tend to part above and below the point of the hock when the horse moves its leg. Use a figure-of-eight bandage instead.

Never kneel on the ground when dealing with a horse's leg; always crouch

1 Make a figure of eight, crossing the bandage over the point of the hock. The first rounds must be tight enough to secure the dressing, but not too tight on the achilles tendon, which runs up the back of the leg above the hock.

2 Finish off the bandage securely. This is especially important with a hock bandage because, if it starts to unravel, the horse will kick out and may re-open the wound.

ROBERT JONES BANDAGE

Life-saving strength

A Robert Jones bandage may save your horse's life. When properly applied, it will immobilise a leg so that even broken bones cannot move. The horse can then be transported for surgery. If a horse will not take any weight on a leg, and you do not know why, apply this bandage immediately so that the problem cannot get any worse.

Use more than one bandage to cover the leg properly

Start the bandage as high up the leg as you can

1 You will need at least four wide rolls of Gamgee and two or three self-adhesive bandages. Wrap the whole leg in two layers of Gamgee, then bandage tightly around them. This stabilises the whole bandage, and ensures that it fits securely around the joints. Then apply two more layers of Gamgee.

2 Next, tightly wrap the whole leg again with a cohesive bandage, which will not come loose. The Gamgee must be tightly compressed.

3 The finished bandage must extend from the top of the leg right down to the hoof to be effective. The horse should be unable to move its leg in a Robert Jones bandage.

ICE PACKS

Applying an ice pack

The application of cold to an inflamed area reduces swelling, heat, and pain. If a horse's leg becomes swollen and you do not know the cause, apply cold to the affected area as your first aid.

1 First, protect the leg with a layer of gauze (half a thickness of Gamgee is fine), so that the ice pack is not in direct contact with the skin. Place the pack directly over and around the swollen area.

PEA PACK

Frozen peas make a good ice pack in an emergency. As the peas thaw, however, the bandage will become loose.

Use a thin layer of padding between the peas and the leg

2 Apply a layer of Gamgee, as insulation to keep the cold in, then bandage the pack in place. The pack may be heavy, so the bandage will need to be quite tight to prevent the pack from moving about on the leg.

COLD HOSING

Simple hosing

Hosing with cold water cools the leg, although not as much as ice. Make sure you stand the horse near a drain.

Hosing boot

A hosing boot holds water fed in from a hose. Fix it to a flexible hose, so it does not restrict movement of the leg too much.

HOT TUBBING

Tubbing the foot

Hot tubbing increases the circulation, bringing more blood cells to the area to fight infection. Clean the horse's foot thoroughly before soaking it in a bowl of hot water for 10–15 minutes. Add Epsom salts to the water to prevent the horn and skin from softening and becoming prone to secondary infection.

APPLYING A POULTICE

Poulticing a foot

A hot poultice provides warmth to the infected area. Chemicals in a ready-made poultice draw fluid and pus out of the wound. Kaolin clay is also effective, but it is messy. In an emergency, use a hot bran mash. A poultice must be changed at least every 12 hours because it loses heat and gets contaminated with pus.

Use safety scissors if you are cutting near a horse

1 Cut the poultice dressing to the approximate size of the foot, allowing an overlap all round.

2 Soak the dressing in warm water – not boiling, which would scald you and the horse. Allow it to drain.

3 Place the dressing over the foot. Fold the edges over the hoof to secure it. It is vital that the poultice does not come off.

4 Use a self-adhesive bandage to keep the dressing in place. Start by wrapping the bandage around the wall of the foot, with about a third of the width projecting below the foot. Make two or three turns around to make sure the bandage is firm.

The projecting part of the bandage will curl over the sole

Do not let the poultice move while you are bandaging

5 Bring the roll of bandage across the sole, and make a further turn around the wall of the foot to secure this length.

Keep the horse's foot off the ground until you have finished bandaging

6 Cross over the sole in the other direction, to produce an "X" of bandage over the sole. Anchor it with another turn around the wall of the foot.

Anchor the bandage with a turn around the foot each time you go across the sole

7 Make as many crosses over the foot as the length of bandage will allow. Smooth down all the edges to stick them firmly to the layers underneath. You have now made a bandage boot.

NURSING A HORSE

When a hospital says that a patient is "comfortable", it does not mean that the person is free from pain, but that everything has been done to make life as pleasant as possible in the circumstances. This is what nursing is all about. When a horse needs nursing, keep it in a large, well-lit, draught-free box. There should be an electricity point and a source of hot water nearby. A sick horse needs constant attention to keep it warm, clean, and, if its condition permits, well fed. You must be on hand to respond to its needs and any change in its condition.

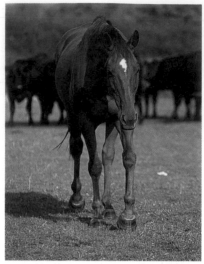

Warning signs
Nursing provides an opportunity for you to study a patient and hopefully find out what is going wrong. Bring a horse in from the field for observation if it does not appear to be eating normally, if it seems lethargic, if it feels colder than you would expect, or if you suspect that it has diarrhoea or is not passing normal droppings.

Giving medicines
These can be mixed with a small amount of the horse's normal feed. If it refuses this, try adding a strong flavour such as molasses, or hiding the drug in a hollowed-out apple or carrot.

Many medicines now come as granules rather than powder

Tuck the towel carefully over the noseband to keep in the steam

Place the bowl on something, such as an upturned bin, so that it is at the right height for the horse

Steam inhalation
A horse's nostrils and airways can become clogged with mucus. A steam inhalation will loosen the mucus and soften any crusting, which might be uncomfortable. Put a few drops of a vapour inhalant into a bowl of hot water. Wrap a towel around the bowl and loosely around the horse's muzzle, so that the horse can breathe only the air containing the medicated steam.

A build-up of straw under the belly restricts movement

Feeling the ears

You can tell whether a horse is feeling cold by feeling its ears gently. Some horses also enjoy being fussed in this way. If the horse is cold, put on a rug. (The ears will not show you if the horse has a high temperature or not.)

Providing adequate bedding

Give a sick horse a good bed to lie on, but do not make it too thick, especially if it is straw. If a horse stands miserably shifting its feet, it may build up a pile of straw between its legs that makes further movement difficult. If this starts to happen, move the horse and redistribute the straw.

Keep a rug over the horse's back to prevent it from catching a chill

Normal routine

Horses like routine, and when they are ill this is all the more important. Give meals and do other tasks at the normal times. Grooming is vital, even for very sick horses; it really freshens them up. If possible, keep the horse within sight of its usual companions and have it nursed by its regular groom.

Disinfection

If a horse has an infectious disease, dip its grooming kit in diluted disinfectant after every use, to prevent the spread of infection.

Chapter 7

TACK AND CLOTHING

H ORSE TACK and
clothing tend to be
expensive, which is one reason
why you should look after
them. A more important reason
to keep them clean and in good
condition is that failure to do so
will be detrimental to the horse. Dirt causes skin
problems; ill-fitting tack, rugs, and
boots are uncomfortable for the
horse and may cause an accident
if they move or come off
suddenly. It may seem a bother
to use tack and clothing correctly,
rather than fasten the straps just anyhow, but
your horse will be more comfortable if you do,
and will follow your requests more willingly.

SADDLES AND GIRTHS

Both horse and rider benefit from a saddle. It stops the horse's spine from digging into the rider, and spreads the rider's weight evenly across the horse's back, avoiding the spine. Saddles are built around a frame called a tree. Protect the tree by storing a saddle on a rack. If the tree breaks, the saddle is useless and hurts the horse. Buy the best saddle you can afford. The best ones are made of leather. Part-fabric or synthetic saddles are cheaper, but do not last as long. If you buy a second-hand saddle, make sure the tree, stitching, and leather are in good repair.

THE SADDLE

Cantle

Seat

Panel

Saddle rack

Under the skirt

Stirrup bar to which stirrup leathers are attached

Waist

Pommel

Stud

Skirt

Types of saddle
There are different types of saddle for different purposes, such as jumping or dressage, and general-purpose saddles for non-specialist riders. Western saddles are ornate, because they were a cowboy's status symbol, and heavy, because they had to withstand the stresses imposed when a lariat was attached to the horn in front of the rider.

Saddle flap

General-purpose saddle (side view)

Cantle

Seat

Horn

Flank girth billet

Fender

Cinch bar

Front tie strap (cinch strap)

Western saddle

Stirrup

Cinch

General-purpose saddle (underside)

Sweat flap

Girth straps

Panel

Gullet

Saddle flap

EXTRA PADDING

Saddle cloth
A saddle cloth keeps the underside of the saddle clean and absorbs sweat, which would otherwise allow the saddle to slip around and rub the horse. It can be made from a variety of materials, but some synthetic materials do not absorb moisture well.

Numnah
A form of padded saddle cloth, a numnah is used to protect the horse's back as well as to absorb sweat. It is usually cut in the shape of a saddle. Do not use one as permanent padding for a poorly fitting or badly stuffed saddle – such a saddle should be replaced or restuffed.

Gel pad
A pad made of thermoplastic elastomer gel ensures an even contact between horse and saddle, and is good for a horse with a sore back. The gel distributes pressure so that it is applied evenly all over.

GIRTHS

Leather girth
Leather is strong and does not stretch much, but it collects sweat and dirt. This makes the girth hard and uncomfortable for the horse if not kept clean. This Balding girth is one of several types. It is designed to be narrow behind the horse's elbow without losing strength.

Three separate pieces can move over each other, making the girth more comfortable for the horse

Two buckles spread the tension evenly and ensure a back-up if one breaks

String girth
A nylon string girth lets air through, and grips better than leather, so it is less likely to rub and cause galls. It will not last as long as a leather girth.

String girths are not as strong as leather, so they are usually wider

It is important to check that the girth is flat when it is done up, and that no skin is trapped between the strings

BRIDLES AND BITS

The bridle enables the rider to control the horse's head. There are two basic kinds of bridle: the snaffle bridle with a single rein, and the double bridle. This has two bits – a bridoon, which is a type of snaffle, and a curb bit – with a rein each. Most bridles are made of leather. You should aim to ride your horse in the simplest bridle and bit possible. A double bridle should be used only to give you more precise control over a willing and well-trained horse, not as a means of controlling an unwilling one.

THE BRIDLE

The parts of a snaffle bridle

This simple bridle consists of one set of reins, a headpiece and throatlash, a browband, a noseband, two cheekpieces, and a bit. The separate pieces can be taken apart for cleaning, for attaching a different type of noseband or bit, or for substituting a piece that fits better.

Headpiece lies on top of the headpiece of the noseband

Reins are in two pieces joined with a central buckle

Headpiece of the noseband threads through the browband

Cheekpiece is attached to the headpiece and the bit

Throatlash

Browband

Cavesson noseband

Cheekpiece

Snaffle bit

Reins are attached to the rings of the bit with the fastenings on the inside

Storing

When off the horse, the bridle should be hung from the headpiece. It is best to use a broad, circular or semi-circular support so that the leather is not bent too sharply. Do not store the bridle, or any tack, in a damp place, because the leather will go mouldy and deteriorate.

Thread the throatlash through the reins and buckle it up

Bridle fitted to the horse

Cavesson noseband fits under the cheekpieces

Throatlash fastens on the near side

Wrap the noseband around the cheekpieces and secure by the keepers

Hang the reins symmetrically

Bit must be attached the right way round so that when in the mouth it will fit over the horse's tongue and not pinch it

Drop noseband

This is used only with a snaffle bit. It stops a horse from getting its tongue over the bit and from opening its mouth wide. It must sit above the nostrils so that it does not restrict breathing.

Cheekpiece must be in front of the line of the lips

Noseband fastens snugly below the bit and rests in the chin groove

Western bridle

The reins are not fastened together, so that one rein can be quickly used to lead or tie the horse. The bit can be severe, but the rider aims for perfect control by training rather than by force.

Curb bit used on its own

Curb strap

Hackamore

This bitless bridle can be used on a horse whose mouth is too sore to take a bit. It has a severe action on the muzzle, so it is also sometimes used on a difficult horse. It should not be used by novice riders.

The long arms exert powerful leverage on the poll

BITS

Action of the bit

The bit fits over the tongue and rests on the bars of the mouth. Many bits have been designed, each claiming to be best in certain situations. Use the simplest bit you can. Usually, the thicker and smoother the mouthpiece, the kinder it is. The most common bit is the single-jointed snaffle. It acts on the bars, the corners of the mouth, and the tongue.

Smooth side-joint

Eggbutt snaffle

As well as being one of the simplest bits, the eggbutt snaffle is perhaps the kindest. The joints between the rings and the mouthpiece are designed not to pinch the horse's lips.

Single-jointed steel mouthpiece

Loose-ring snaffle

This type of snaffle is another simple bit. The rings can move freely through the mouthpiece, but there is a danger that they may trap and pinch the corners of the mouth.

Vulcanite mouthpiece gives a "softer" feeling than steel

Mullen-mouth snaffle

The straight bar can be made of steel, vinyl, vulcanite, or rubber. The horse can soften its effect by pressing upwards with its tongue.

Curb chain

Mullen-mouth pelham

A pelham bit is used instead of two bits in a double bridle. It is used with a curb chain, which acts on the chin groove.

Port, or tongue groove

Kimblewick

The "ported" mouthpiece of this single-rein pelham puts pressure on the roof of the mouth, but allows more room for the tongue.

FITTING TACK

It is in the interests of both horse and rider that the tack fits properly. If it does not, it will be painful for the horse, which may lead to it resisting the aids given by the rider. A saddle should be specific to a horse. You may need to have one made to measure for some horses, to ensure that it fits perfectly. Loose-fitting tack may fail to pass a given signal to the horse, or may come off, causing a serious accident. If you have any doubts about the equipment you are using, consult an expert from your local saddlery.

THE SADDLE

The saddle must be fitted without a saddle cloth or numnah

The saddle should not be so long that it puts weight on the horse's loins

Position
The saddle should lie straight on the horse's back, resting on the ribs, not the spine. The sides of the horse's chest are nearly parallel at this point, and this helps to keep the saddle in place.

Space through the gullet
When the horse's head is down, you should be able to see right through the gullet. The gullet is designed to keep weight off the horse's spine.

Check that you can see through the gullet when the girth is done up and when a rider is sitting on the horse

Chalk mark test
Dust the saddle's underside with chalk and place it on the horse. When you remove it, a chalk mark will show if the saddle touches the horse where it shouldn't.

Correct width
A saddle must be the same width as the horse's shoulders. If it is too narrow, it will pinch the spine and restrict movement. If it is too wide, it will be low on the withers.

Height of the pommel
The pommel lies over the withers. It must be high enough to allow the horse to lift its head right up without the withers pressing against the pommel.

Snug fit
A well-fitting saddle sits securely even before the girth is fastened. If it moves about too much while you are riding, it will rub the horse's back.

THE BRIDLE

Tightness of the noseband

A cavesson noseband is done up loosely, with room for two fingers between it and the nose. A drop noseband should be tighter, because it is meant to keep the bit in place and stop the horse from opening its mouth too wide.

Level of the noseband

The noseband should lie about midway between the mouth and the projecting cheekbones. You should be able to fit two fingers below the cheekbone. The sidepieces of the noseband must not touch the horse's eyes.

The throatlash helps to keep the bridle in place

Throatlash

The throatlash must be long enough to allow four fingers between it and the horse when it is done up. If it is tighter, it can interfere with the horse's breathing.

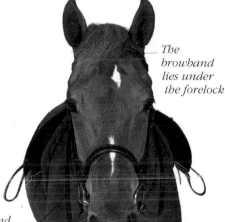

The browband lies under the forelock

Browband

You should be able to fit two fingers under the browband. It must not pull the headpiece and cheekpieces, but should allow them to lie in a straight line.

The noseband sits on the bridge of the nose

Front view

Look carefully at the bridle on the horse's head from the front. Make sure that it is straight and positioned symmetrically on both sides.

Fitting the bit correctly

A badly fitting bit will be uncomfortable for the horse and can injure the mouth. All bits should lie in the corners of the mouth without wrinkling the lips too much. The horse should look as if it is smiling. If the bit is too high it will rub the corners of the mouth; if it is too low, it may hit the teeth. The mouthpiece should protrude 5 mm (¼ in) on each side when you hold the joint straight in the mouth. If it is too wide, it will move from side to side and rub; too narrow, and it will pinch the lips.

Correct fit

Too high

Too low

Too wide

Too narrow

PUTTING ON A SADDLE

You should not tack up a horse until you are ready to ride. Brush off any stable or sweat marks, and any dry mud, especially where the saddle and girth will be. Put the saddle on first. Some horses appear to expand their belly when the saddle is first put on but later relax, leaving the girth loose. By the time you have put on the bridle, the horse will have relaxed and you can then tighten the girth before you mount. Do not leave a horse standing with its saddle on when you have finished riding. If it wants to roll, it will do so even with the saddle in place. This may not only damage the saddle but also hurt the horse's back.

The horse should be tied up securely while you tack up

Stand close to the horse

1 Approach the horse slowly, talking to it all the time. Smooth down the hair on the back, then lay the saddle cloth over the withers and saddle area.

Put the cloth further forward than the final position of the saddle, to allow you to move it and the saddle back together later, in the direction of the lie of the coat.

2 Check that the stirrups are run up, and that the girth is fastened on one side and folded over the saddle. Place the saddle on the cloth, lowering it vertically so that you do not move the cloth. Do not pull the saddle or cloth forwards, because this will rub the horse's hair the wrong way.

3 Hold the saddle cloth well up in the arch and gullet of the saddle, then move the saddle and saddle cloth backwards together until the saddle sits in its correct position behind the withers. Attach the saddle cloth to the saddle by threading the middle girth strap through the loop provided on the cloth.

Bring the girth down gently; do not throw it over from the other side

You must use the same two straps on both sides of the saddle

5 Walk back around the horse and fasten the girth. Attach one buckle to the front strap. This strap is fixed to the saddle separately so that if it breaks, the other one will hold the girth, and vice versa. Pull the girth tight without wrinkling the skin.

4 Walk around the front of the horse to the other side, going under the neck if necessary. Hang the girth down, then check that everything is lying flat.

6 Pull the buckle guards down over the buckles of the girth. This stops the buckles from moving about or digging into your legs while you are riding, and prevents them from rubbing and damaging the saddle.

The girth should lie slightly in front of an imaginary vertical line drawn through the centre of the saddle

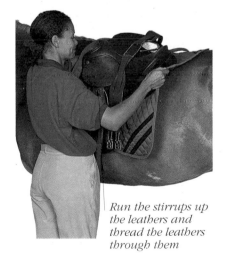

Run the stirrups up the leathers and thread the leathers through them

Removing the saddle
Undo the girth on one side, then cross it over the saddle. Take hold of both saddle and saddle cloth and lift them off together, moving them backwards slightly as you do so.

7 After you have checked and tightened the girth, pull each foreleg forwards to make sure that no skin is wrinkled under the girth. If the horse reacts as you tighten the girth, it may be a bad habit but it could be because of a back problem or a painful saddle.

PUTTING ON A BRIDLE

Put the bridle on after the saddle. Carry it on one arm by the headpiece and the reins, with the browband pointing towards your elbow. Make sure you will be able to put it on without having to untangle it or untwist straps. Approach the horse from the front, so that it can see what you have in your hands. Try not to let a metal bit clink as you walk, because some horses will react to the noise. Always have some means of restraint on the horse's head or neck while you are putting on the bridle so that you can stop it from walking off. Do not let the horse escape from you with the bridle hanging half on, because it could easily get a leg caught in the reins.

The stirrups should always be run up until you are ready to mount

1 Untie the horse, then undo the headcollar, slip it off the horse's muzzle, and fasten it around the neck. Stand on the left of the horse, take the reins in your right hand, and put them over its head. Alternatively, you could put the reins over the head, then remove the headcollar.

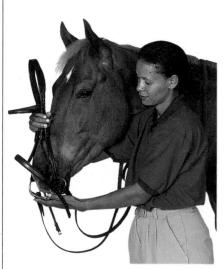

2 Put your right arm under the horse's jaw and hold the cheekpieces of the bridle together in front of its face. Rest the bit on your left hand, just under the muzzle. The noseband will encircle the horse's jaws.

3 Move the bridle gently up the horse's face. When the bit touches the horse's mouth, insert your thumb gently between the lips at the corner, so that it presses slightly on the gum in the gap between the horse's teeth. This should encourage the horse to open its mouth.

5 Check that all the parts of the bridle are lying straight and flat before fastening the buckles. Do the throatlash up first, so that if the horse pulls away from you it will not pull the bridle off. It is the throatlash that keeps the bridle on. Do it up loosely (see p. 159).

4 Bring the headpiece up over the horse's ears, taking care not to let the bit drop out of the horse's mouth. Carefully fit both ears between the browband and the headpiece, and check that all the horse's forelock is lying free over the browband.

6 Finally, fasten the noseband. A cavesson noseband should be done up loosely and lie next to the horse's face, underneath the cheekpieces. A drop noseband should be tighter and lie below the bit (see p. 157).

Put the end of each strap through its keeper and runner

Removing the bridle

When you remove the bridle, first fasten a headcollar loosely around the horse's neck. Undo the noseband and then the throatlash on the bridle. Bring the reins up the horse's neck, and take hold of them and the headpiece in one hand. Pull them all gently over the ears, and lower the bridle slowly down the front of the horse's face. The horse will ease the bit out of its mouth, and the noseband will fall away of its own accord. Do not pull the bridle off too quickly and bang the bit against the horse's teeth.

LEAVING A HORSE TACKED UP SAFELY

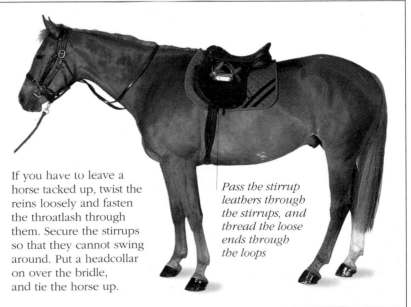

If you have to leave a horse tacked up, twist the reins loosely and fasten the throatlash through them. Secure the stirrups so that they cannot swing around. Put a headcollar on over the bridle, and tie the horse up.

Pass the stirrup leathers through the stirrups, and thread the loose ends through the loops

EXTRA EQUIPMENT

The bridle and saddle are the means by which we stay on the horse and control where it goes, but, in some cases, extra equipment may be needed. For example, some horses have a shape that makes it difficult for them to wear a saddle without it slipping backwards. In such cases, a breast plate or a breast girth may be necessary. There are also horses who throw their heads around; for these horses a martingale is used to restrict their head movements. Take care not to use extra items of tack unless you have first checked that they really are necessary: a breast plate is no substitute for a properly fitting saddle, and you should not use a martingale to mask a painful mouth that causes resentment of the bit.

BREAST PLATE

Features and fitting
A breast plate is a fixed loop that passes around the horse's neck, and is anchored to the saddle by a strap on each side, and to the girth by a strap between the legs. At rest, the breast plate should allow four fingers between it and the horse's shoulder. Check that none of the straps is twisted.

BREAST GIRTH

Features and fitting
A breast girth is a strap that is fixed to the girth on both sides, passing around the breast. A strap over the neck stops it from slipping down around the legs. A breast girth should lie more or less parallel to the ground and, as with the breast plate, should allow four fingers to fit between it and the horse when at rest.

USING A RUNNING MARTINGALE

Make sure that the loop for the girth is facing backwards

1 A running martingale is a strap that attaches to the girth. It is split into two, with a ring on the end of each part through which the reins are allowed to run freely. It is supported by a neck strap. It helps a rider to control a horse that is prone to carry its head too high. When using a running martingale, put the saddle and bridle on first. Pass the neck strap of the martingale over the head and the reins.

2 Unbuckle the girth, and pass it through the loop on the end of the martingale's girth strap. (This loop has a buckle, which you should use to adjust the length of the martingale – see step 3.) Do up the girth of the saddle again.

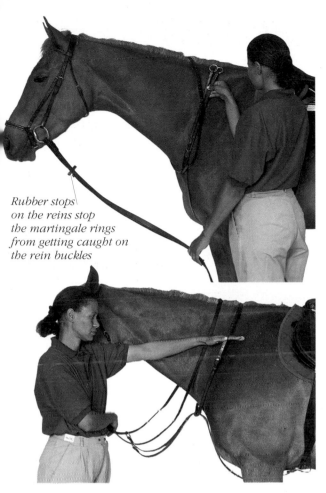

Rubber stops on the reins stop the martingale rings from getting caught on the rein buckles

3 The first time you put on the martingale, check the length of the ringed straps. It is these that apply pressure to the bit via the reins if the horse lifts its head. Adjust the length so that they reach together to the top of the neck near the withers.

4 Separate the reins by undoing the buckle. Thread one rein through each ring, then re-buckle the reins. Make sure that neither the reins nor the martingale straps are twisted.

Use a thick rubber ring, designed for the purpose, to keep the neck strap and martingale together

5 Check that the neck strap allows four fingers between it and the horse's neck. When leading a horse that is wearing a running martingale do not bring the reins over the head, because you will put pressure on the bars of the horse's mouth. For very short distances, hold both reins about 30 cm (12 in) under the horse's chin. Otherwise, unbuckle the reins and tie up the rings, or use a headcollar.

USING A STANDING MARTINGALE

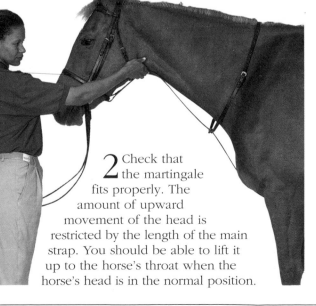

A standing martingale should be used only with a cavesson noseband

1 A standing martingale has one strap that attaches to the girth and the noseband, and a neck strap. It prevents a horse from lifting its head too high. Fix the martingale to the girth in the same way as a running martingale. Pass the noseband through the loop on the martingale strap, and do it up.

2 Check that the martingale fits properly. The amount of upward movement of the head is restricted by the length of the main strap. You should be able to lift it up to the horse's throat when the horse's head is in the normal position.

CLEANING TACK

Keep tack clean, supple, and in good repair. It is especially important that the bit, girth, and saddle cloth are cleaned, otherwise dirt will rub into the horse's skin during riding and cause inflammation and infection. Saddle-soap leather at least once a week, and clean off dirt after every ride. Check for wear, especially of the stitching, as you clean the tack. If it breaks while you are riding, it could cause an accident and injure both you and the horse. Take the bridle apart for a thorough check once a month, even if you do not ride often. Tack can still deteriorate even when it is not being used.

TACK-CLEANING EQUIPMENT

You should keep all your tack-cleaning equipment together, perhaps in a bucket kept solely for cleaning. Keep it really clean, otherwise it will simply transfer dirt back to the tack. The type of sponge you use is particularly important. You need to be able to squeeze it almost dry. Replace it regularly. There is no point in using one that is falling to bits.

Bucket

Saddle soap

Sponge

Stiff brush

Damp cloth

Polishing cloth

Dry cloth

Stable rubber

Metal polish

Brush for oil

Saddle oil

CLEANING THE BRIDLE

Lower the cheekpieces to their lowest hole, noting which hole they were on

Unbuckle the noseband and throatlash

1 Hang the bridle from a firm hook fixed at eye level. Wipe all parts with a damp cloth folded around them. Hold each piece taut with one hand, and rub the cloth up and down it with the other hand. Take care to include stretches of leather that are usually covered by a buckle or runner.

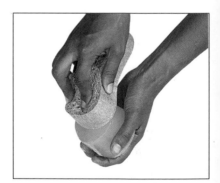

2 Moisten the saddle soap and rub this on a damp sponge. Do not soak the sponge in the water: you will put more water than soap on the leather, and it will dry hard rather than supple.

3 Soap all the leather on both sides by rubbing the sponge up and down. Remember to include the pieces from which the bridle is hanging.

Bit and stirrups

The bit must always be washed after use. Soak it in a bucket of water to wash off dried grass and food. Also soak the stirrup irons, to wash off mud. Remove the stirrup leathers first, and wash the stirrup treads separately if necessary.

Be careful not to put any of the leather in the water – it will damage the leather and any stitching

Polishing metal

Any metal work that shows can be buffed up with metal polish. Do not use polish on the mouthpiece of the bit. It will taste unpleasant and irritate the horse's mouth.

CLEANING THE SADDLE

1 Remove the girth, the buckle guards, if detachable, and the stirrup leathers. Clean a leather girth and the stirrup leathers in the same way as the bridle. Turn the saddle upside down, and clean the panel and the underside first. Then rest the saddle on a saddle-horse while you do the rest. Start by washing off dirt and grease with a damp cloth.

CLEANING NON-LEATHER GIRTHS

Remove mud and hair with a stiff brush, then soak the girth in soapy water and rinse thoroughly. Do not use detergent, because it can irritate the horse's skin. Clean saddle cloths in the same way. Some girths and cloths can be put in a washing machine. They must be completely dry before they are used again.

Brush down in the direction of the strings

2 Apply saddle soap to all leatherwork with a circular motion. Soap all the crevices between the flaps and straps. Do not soap any cloth or suede areas, but brush them to remove dirt.

3 Oil leatherwork periodically to protect it more, especially the rough underside, because this is the most absorbent. Oil only clean leather. Wipe off excess oil, which would stain your clothes.

STABLE RUGS

The top stable door, windows, and air vents should be open all year round in most climates, so a stabled horse, especially one that has been clipped, usually needs to wear a rug during the winter to keep it warm. Once you have started to use a rug at night, do not leave it off, even on milder nights, because the horse could catch a chill; wait until you can leave it off permanently for the season. Stable rugs have two layers, the outer for protection and a lining for warmth. The lining should extend over the whole rug. Check this, because in cheap rugs only half the rug is lined. The outer layer can be made of a variety of materials; the best is linen. There is also a wide range of fastenings, many claiming to hold the rug in place even if the horse rolls.

PUTTING ON A RUG

1 Fold the rug in half front to back with the straps secured inside. Carry it over your arm, with the front half of the rug uppermost and the fold away from you. Approach the left side of the horse, and warn it that you are about to put the rug on by placing your free hand on its shoulder.

2 Throw the folded rug over the horse's withers. Place it so that the front is just a little further forward than its final position. Unfold the rug over the quarters, then pull it backwards and check that it is lying straight over the back of the horse.

Cross the straps under the belly

Fastening a strap

3 Go around to the other side of the horse to bring down the straps and check that the rug is flat. Return to the near side to do up the rug. Fasten the belly straps first. If the horse escapes, it may panic if the rug slips and hangs around its neck.

4 Fasten the breast straps. If the rug is too far forward, pull it backwards slightly. If it is too far back for the breast straps to be fastened, take it off and start again. Never pull a rug forwards; this rubs the coat hairs the wrong way and causes discomfort.

The correct size

Rugs come in a wide range of sizes, measured along the length. Measure your horse for a rug from the centre of its breastbone along its side to the point of the buttock. A rug must reach from the withers to the top of the tail. When it is on, you should be able to fit a hand sideways under it at the shoulder and at the breast, without disturbing its position.

Correct fit at shoulder

The rug must not be too tight, because it will rub the horse

Correct fit at breast

PUTTING ON AN UNDERBLANKET AND A ROLLER

1 If you need to provide extra warmth for a horse, use a blanket under the rug. Place the blanket as far up the horse's neck as possible, with the rear edge reaching the tail. Fold the front corners up to meet on the horse's spine.

2 Check that the blanket is lying flat and hanging evenly on both sides, then put the rug in place. Take care to position the rug correctly without disturbing the blanket underneath. Fold the exposed triangle of blanket from the neck over on top of the rug. This helps to stop the blanket from slipping.

If you use a jute rug, such as this one, choose one with as close a weave as possible

Use a breast girth, especially on a very fit horse or one with a narrow chest, to prevent the roller from slipping backwards

Do the roller up as tight as you would a girth

3 When using a rug that has no belly straps, secure it with a roller and breast girth. Fasten the roller around the horse, just behind the withers. Rollers come in different styles. Some may need extra padding over the spine, such as a piece of sponge placed between them and the rug.

OTHER RUGS

There are a variety of rugs, which are used mainly to keep a horse warm or as protection from bad weather. Take care when fitting a new rug, especially a New Zealand or all-in-one rug: the stiffness of the material or the slight hindrance of movement can upset some horses. Rugs must not be used when dirty. Wash them regularly, including the straps, in a non-biological washing agent, and rinse and dry them thoroughly.

NEW ZEALAND RUG

A New Zealand rug must be long enough to protect the horse's underside from wind and rain

Main features

The New Zealand rug is designed to be worn in a field to give protection from wind and cold. It is not totally waterproof and, when soaked, is heavy and cumbersome. The fit of this rug is particularly important, because the material does not mould well to a horse's shape.

Leg straps
There are two straps in front of the hind legs. Pass each one around the leg and attach it to the underside of the rug on the same side. Pass the second strap through the loop of the first one.

Fixed like this, the straps hold each other away from the thigh so they do not rub

The smooth side of the clip must lie next to the horse

Checking a turned-out horse
Keep an eye on a horse that is turned out in a rug, in case the rug slips out of place. If it does slip, take it right off and put it back on. If you just pull it back into place, you will rub the horse's coat the wrong way. The horse must be tied up while you remove and put on the rug, otherwise it might gallop off with the rug half on.

MORE TYPES OF RUG

All-in-one rug

Most all-in-one rugs are completely waterproof. They are much lighter and more flexible than traditional New Zealand rugs, and provide protection for the head and neck. Some horses resent a head cover at first, so give them time to get used to it before turning them out.

When worn under a light rug, the mesh allows air pockets to form, which insulate against the cold

This rug is shaped to follow the lines of the horse to give a better fit

Sweat sheet

This mesh rug is used after hard work to provide some warmth against the cooling effect of sweating whilst still allowing the sweat to evaporate. A sweat sheet may be used, secured with a roller, both in the stable and out in the field.

A fillet string, which runs around the back of the hindquarters under the tail, must be used to prevent the rug from blowing forwards

Exercise sheet

Fitted under the saddle, this provides warmth for a clipped horse during slow work. It covers the hindquarters but leaves the shoulders free for movement. An exercise sheet should not be used in fast work, because it will prevent sweat from evaporating and may cause muscles to overheat.

Summer sheet

This is really the summer version of a New Zealand rug, and is made from lightweight material. The sheet is not at all waterproof, but it may provide welcome protection from flies and can be used to keep a horse clean. The surcingles, or straps, go from front to back, crossing under the belly, to hold down the light material in the wind.

PROTECTIVE BOOTS

Boots for horses are not fitted over the feet, but are attached to the legs to protect them from injury during exercise. They must be fastened tight enough to prevent chafing, as movement will rub any dirt into the skin and start an infection. They should be taken off after work. There are a variety of makes of boot available, in a variety of materials. Beware of "scientific" boots that claim to help the horse withstand the stresses of work. Nothing strapped to the leg will do that.

Brushing boots
As the name implies, this type of boot is worn to prevent brushing (see p. 127). It should be fitted so that the straps are on the outside, and the major protective face is on the inside. It should be worn as one of a pair.

Brushing boot

Correctly fitted brushing boots

Tendon boots
These are designed to provide extra protection to the tendons whilst restricting movement as little as possible. If the horse damages them during fast work they should be thrown away and a new pair used, because the horse is likely to hit itself again in the same place.

Tendon boot

The two padded areas should go on either side of the tendons

Inside of tendon boot

Straps on the outside, facing backwards

Correctly fitted tendon boots

Over-reach boots
These boots protect the heel and the lower part of the pastern. Some types are circular, and are pulled on over the foot, while others are open and fastened around the pastern. They are loose-fitting, but must not be too long, which is dangerous because the horse can tread on them. They should just cover the bulb of the heel but not be touching the ground. Remember, they will be nearer the ground in fast work.

One-piece over-reach boot

Petal over-reach boot

Open petal boot

Correctly fitted over-reach boots

Sausage boot

These rings come in different sizes. Large ones are used on an injured leg in the stable. When the horse lies down, the boot lifts the foot and leg off the ground, protecting the pastern, fetlock, and elbow from knocks. Small ones can be worn during exercise on a hind leg, as shown here, to prevent brushing.

Sausage boot

Correctly fitted
sausage boot

Knee
boot

Knee boot

There is a variety of designs of knee boot, but all have a large protective pad for the front of the knee. The straps going around the back of the leg are minimal, so as to restrict movement as little as possible.

Correctly fitted knee boots

Travelling boots

Used only during travelling, these protect the leg from the knee or hock down to the foot. They are used to provide padding, rather than protection from hard knocks sustained at speed, so are made from soft materials.

Travelling boot for front leg

Correctly
fitted front boots

Travelling boot for hind leg

Correctly
fitted hind boots

PUTTING ON TRAVELLING BOOTS

1 Wrap the boot around the leg, with the straps on the outside and pointing backwards. Place it slightly higher than its final position, with the shaped parts above the joints they are designed to fit. Fasten the middle strap around the leg, to hold the boot in place.

2 Next, slide the boot downwards so that the fetlock and the knee or hock fit into the appropriate parts of the boot, and the top of the hoof is covered. Fasten the lower straps, keeping the pressure even all the way down.

3 Fasten the top straps. The horse will not be doing anything more than a gentle walk, so the boots need to be fastened just tight enough to keep them in place. Finally, check the centre strap again. It may now seem too loose.

TAIL AND LEG BANDAGES

It is sometimes necessary to use bandages on a horse in circumstances other than first aid. A tail bandage is used to keep the tail clean and prevent the hairs from being rubbed off or caught up on something, especially during travelling (see p. 70). It can also be used after grooming to encourage the hairs to lie flat (see p. 61). Leg bandages are used to provide support, protection from injury, or warmth. They should never be used without some padding between the leg and the bandage. The padding provides extra warmth and helps to keep the pressure even. The method of fastening bandages varies according to the make; tapes and Velcro fastenings are common. Keep all your bandages clean by washing them carefully and rinsing them thoroughly. They must be perfectly dry before you use them again.

BANDAGES AND PADDING

Types of bandage
Tail bandages are fairly thin, and are made of crepe or synthetic material. Exercise bandages are slightly elastic, to enable them to mould to the shape of the legs. Stable bandages are thick, felt-like leg bandages designed to provide warmth rather than fit.

Tail bandage
7–10 cm (3–4 in) wide

Stable bandage
10 cm (4 in) wide

Exercise bandage
7 cm (3 in) wide

Types of padding
Fibregee can become compacted and lose its padding ability with repeated use, but it is easier to shape around the leg than Gamgee and more hard wearing. Fibregee can be washed to extend its life, but Gamgee cannot be washed.

Fibregee

Gamgee

PUTTING ON A TAIL BANDAGE

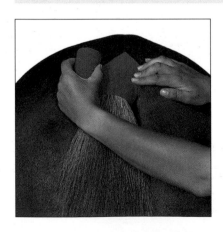

1 Start bandaging with the straight end forming a point across the base of the tail. Wrap the bandage under and around the tail, keeping it as close to the base as possible.

2 Fold the point over the first circle of bandage and cover it with the second layer. Be sure that the bandage is secure at the top, because this will ensure that the finished bandage stays on.

3 Work your way down the tail, overlapping every layer half or two-thirds of the width of the previous layer. Keep the tension firm and even, but not too tight or the bandage will cut off the circulation.

4 Bandage the tail as far down as the tail bones (the dock) extend. This will usually be as far as the groin area at the top of the legs. Then bandage back up the tail.

5 The bandage may have two tapes at the end. Separate them, keeping tension on the one pointing away from the bandage or the last layers will come loose.

6 Cross the tapes behind the tail, keeping them flat. Tie them with a bow at the front, being careful to tie them at the same tension as the bandage.

7 Fold a layer of bandage down over the loops and loose ends of the tapes to give a tidy finish. This should also stop the tapes from coming undone.

8 Lift the bandaged tail and place an arm underneath it as a fulcrum. Gently bend the tail over the arm. This will help it to sit snugly over the horse's buttocks rather than stick rigidly straight out behind.

Removing a tail bandage
Never leave a tail bandage on for more than a few hours, because it can stop the circulation to the tail. When you remove it, untie the tapes, then grasp the sides of the bandage at the top and pull downwards with a sharp tug. The tail narrows towards the tip, so the bandage will come off easily.

LEG BANDAGES

Using leg bandages

Stable bandages can be used as support, or to protect veterinary dressings from dirt and from the horse. They can also be used instead of boots (see p. 173) for protection when travelling. Exercise bandages can be used to protect the legs, especially the tendons, from knocks during exercise. Take great care when putting on leg bandages. If they are too tight, they can damage the tendons. If they are too loose, they will fall off and get trapped around the horse's feet.

Stable bandage

Always bandage a pair of legs, even if only one is injured, to stop one leg from taking more strain than the other. For travelling, make sure that each bandage extends right down over the coronet band.

Exercise bandage

The bandages should start just below the knee or hock, and extend to just above the fetlock joint. Ask an expert to help you put them on. Remove them immediately after use.

PUTTING ON A STABLE BANDAGE

The vertical edges must avoid the tendons

Have the body of bandage on top

Bandage anticlockwise on the near legs, clockwise on the off legs

1 Wrap padding around the leg, keeping it flat. Overlap it so that the outer edge goes anticlockwise on the near legs and clockwise on the off legs.

2 Start at the top. Lay the end of the bandage to form a point at the top, then wrap it around twice, from front to back, in the same direction as the padding.

3 Fold the point down over the turns of bandage, and cover it with another layer to anchor it. Do not pull too hard, or the bandage will move around the leg.

Bring the bandage up at an angle as you start to work back up the leg

Do not let creases form in the bandage or the padding underneath

4 Continue bandaging down the leg, keeping a firm, constant pressure. Overlap each layer about two-thirds of the one above. Take care to maintain the overlaps over the fetlock joint.

5 Work back up the leg. Form a V-shape at the front of the leg between the last layer of bandage going down and the first layer going up. This stops the bandage from moving as the horse moves.

6 Aim to finish the bandage just below the starting point. The fastening may be a Velcro strap or tapes to tie. Try to fasten it on the outside of the leg, so that it does not rub against the other leg.

Removing a leg bandage
Do not attempt to roll the bandage up as you remove it. You cannot expect the horse to stand still patiently while you do so. Undo the fastening, then pass the bandage from hand to hand as you unwind it. Try not to let the padding fall on the floor.

ROLLING UP A BANDAGE

You must roll up a bandage properly so that it is the right way round when you use it. Start at the end that has the strap or tapes. Fold it over, then roll the bandage firmly with the fastening on the inside. Align the edges neatly.

Chapter 8

HINTS AND TIPS

THE HORSE WORLD is
full of technical terms.
To make sure that you
know what many of them
mean, this section includes a
comprehensive glossary
where they are briefly
explained. There are pointers
on what to look for when buying a
horse, tips on how to organize your time when you
own a horse, and guidelines for choosing a livery
should you need to. You cannot be expected to
know everything about horse care, and the list of
useful addresses will show you where to obtain
further information. Never be
embarrassed to ask for help; your
ignorance may harm the horse.

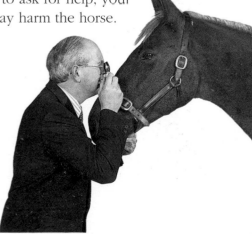

ALL-YEAR-ROUND CARE

The life of a wild horse might seem boring to you, because every day is basically the same, but the horse is designed in the expectation that every day will be like the others. The domesticated horse must have a regular routine, too, to avoid problems such as colic and azoturia. The best routine is one that you can stick to 365 days a year. It has to fit in with weekday activities such as work or school without changing drastically at the weekends. If you change it, do so gradually.

IDENTIFICATION CODING

Being able to prove the identity of your horse makes it easier to recover it if it is stolen, and makes the horse less desirable to the thief. There are a number of ways you can achieve this. Hoof-branding with your post code allows you to be traced immediately as the horse's owner. The brand needs to be renewed as the hooves grow. Freeze-branding a code on the horse's body is permanent. It uses irons cooled in liquid nitrogen and is less painful than hot branding. The hair grows white to show the code. In electronic tagging, a microchip is inserted under the horse's skin and transmits a code when activated by a scanner. The tag cannot be seen or easily removed.

Freeze-brand

Hoof-brand

POSSIBLE ROUTINES FOR KEEPING A HORSE AT GRASS

DAILY		
	Summer	**Winter**
Early	Catch the horse and check for any injuries. Pick out feet, and wipe any discharge from the eyes before it attracts flies. Check water source, or refill a bucket with fresh water. Feed concentrate if necessary.	Catch horse and check for injury. Check feet for signs of disorders. Check rug, changing for clean, dry one if necessary. Check that water is not frozen. Feed hay, and concentrate if necessary.
Mid-morning	Catch horse for riding. Lightly groom and tack up. On return from riding, untack the horse and wipe down. Pick out feet, put on fly repellant or fringe if necessary, and turn out. Feed if necessary.	Remove rug, lightly groom, and tack up. Replace rug after riding, pick out feet, and turn horse out. Feed hay, and concentrate if necessary. Check that boundaries are secure, and remove rubbish.
Afternooon	Feed concentrate if necessary. Check water source. Check that field boundaries are secure, and remove any rubbish or large stones. Clean tack.	Catch horse. Adjust rug, and check underneath for rubs. Pick out feet and turn out. Feed hay, and concentrate if necessary. Check water supply. Clean tack.
Evening	Catch horse and check for any signs of lameness or injury. Pick out feet and turn out again. Check water supply. Feed concentrate if necessary.	Catch horse, and check for any signs of lameness or injury. Adjust rug, and turn out again. Feed hay, and concentrate if necessary. Check water supply.

WEEKLY	**MONTHLY**	**YEARLY**
Remove droppings from field. Check field for poisonous plants and remove and burn. Check feed supply. Strip-clean tack. Check first-aid kit.	Top the paddock during the growing season. Check dates of next worming and next visit from farrier. Clean water buckets and troughs.	Arrange dental check and tetanus and flu vaccinations. Apply preservative to fencing and shelters. Clear ditches. Follow pasture maintenance procedure.

POSSIBLE ROUTINES FOR KEEPING A HORSE STABLED

DAILY		
	Summer	**Winter**
Early	Check horse all over, and pick out feet. Fill haynet, and feed concentrate if necessary. Give fresh water. Muck out stable.	As summer, but also remove and replace rug and any blanket with lighter rug. Check for rubs. Deal with any ice and snow in the stableyard.
Mid-morning	Groom lightly to remove stable stains and make horse comfortable. Tack up and exercise. On return, remove tack and groom thoroughly. Fill haynet, and feed concentrate if necessary. Check water supply.	As summer, but remove any sweat after exercise, and dry thoroughly before replacing rug.
Afternoon	Remove droppings. Check hay and water. Tack up and exercise. (If not possible, trot horse up and down to stretch its legs and check it for lameness.) Feed concentrate if necessary. Clean tack.	As summer, but check position of rug, and for any rubs, if horse is not being ridden.
Evening	Remove droppings and shake up bed. Feed concentrate if necessary. Pick out feet. Check water and fill haynet. Give final check of horse last thing and check security of stableyard.	As summer, but replace day rug with usual night rug for extra warmth at night.

WEEKLY	MONTHLY	YEARLY
Check feed supply. Strip clean tack. Clean rugs. Remove cobwebs from upper stable walls. Check first-aid kit. Clean stable equipment.	Check bedding supply. Check date of next worming and next shoeing. Check drains and guttering. Clean waterers and mangers.	Arrange manure disposal, flu and tetanus vaccinations, and dental check. Check fire extinguishers. Do major maintenance jobs such as painting.

POSSIBLE ROUTINES USING THE COMBINED SYSTEM

DAILY		
	Summer (horse in during the day, out at night)	**Winter (horse in at night, out during the day)**
Early	Catch horse and put in stable. Check all over, and pick out feet. Fill haynet, check water supply, and feed concentrate if necessary.	Check horse all over, and pick out feet. Adjust rugs. Fill haynet, and feed concentrate if necessary. Change water, and remove droppings.
Mid-morning	Groom horse lightly, tack up, and exercise. On return, untack and clean off sweat. Remove droppings, and check water supply. Fill haynet, and feed concentrate if necessary.	Groom horse lightly, tack up, and exercise. On return, untack, rub down, and put on field rug. Pick out feet, and turn out. Feed hay, and concentrate if necessary. Check water in field.
Afternoon	Remove droppings and check water. Fill haynet, and feed concentrate if necessary. Clean tack. Check that field boundaries are secure.	Muck out stable. Clean tack. Check horse and rug. Feed hay, and concentrate if necessary. Check field boundaries.
Evening	Feed concentrate if necessary. Check horse for lameness, pick out feet, and turn out. Check water in field. Muck out stable, and check stableyard security.	Catch horse and bring in. Change rug. Give fresh water, and concentrate if necessary. Fill haynet. Give final check of horse last thing, and check stableyard security.

BUYING AND KEEPING A HORSE

Before you look for a horse to buy, you must make definite arrangements about where and how you are going to keep it. Apart from anything else, this will affect the type and size of horse that you can have; if you have only a small stable and paddock, you will not be able to accommodate a large horse. You can care for your horse yourself or keep it at livery (which means that you rent facilities). The most expensive way to keep a horse is to have it at "full livery". The horse is fed, stabled, groomed, and maybe exercised by the staff. Other forms of livery include "do it yourself" and partial livery.

VIEWING A HORSE

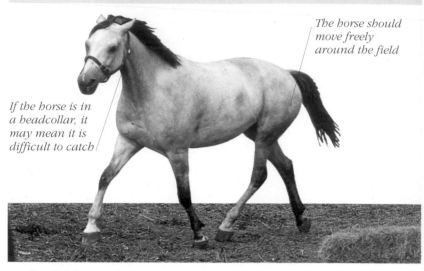

The horse should move freely around the field

If the horse is in a headcollar, it may mean it is difficult to catch

In the field
When buying a horse, ask the owner if you can see it loose in the field first. Watch its body language as it approaches both you and other horses, to spot signs of aggression or timidity. Make sure that you are able to catch it easily on your own.

In the stable
See what sort of bedding is used and why. If the horse needs different bedding from the other horses, this may indicate respiratory problems. Watch for signs of stable vices such as weaving.

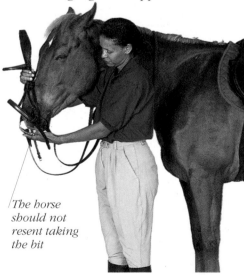

The horse should not resent taking the bit

Tacking up
Tack the horse up yourself before riding it to see how it behaves. Make sure that it stands still and that its back does not sink down when you fasten the girth. An adverse reaction by a horse to being tacked up may mean that you will have problems later.

The vet will check the horse's teeth to assess its age

Veterinary examination
Always have the horse thoroughly checked over by a vet before purchase. The examination will cover every aspect of the horse's health. The vet will advise you of any defect that the horse has, and how it may affect the work that you want the horse to do.

KEEPING A HORSE AT LIVERY

A tidy stableyard
The overall discipline that results in a tidy stableyard may ensure a good, regular routine for your horse. Look around the yard for clues such as a neat muck heap, tack that is clean and in good condition, and well-shod horses.

Choosing a livery yard
When choosing a livery yard for your horse, it is more important to learn about the people that work there rather than the buildings. Spend some time watching the staff; are they kind to the horses? Do they seem to work efficiently? Is the tack clean and in good condition?

Livery will be cheaper if you do tasks such as tack cleaning yourself

Grazing facilities
Whether you keep your horse at home or at livery, it ought to have access to grazing land. The paddocks should be safe (see p. 76) and, even in winter, there should be some grass around rather than just bare ground. Horses prefer to graze with company rather than alone; make sure that your horse will have amenable, rather than hostile, companions.

Responsibility for routine tasks
It is important to have set down in writing the services that will be provided by the livery yard, and which of these will be charged for separately. For example, will you have to clean your own tack? Who will organize the worming of your horse, and who will pay for the wormer? Equipment such as rugs and grooming kit, which you may have to provide, can also be a significant extra cost.

GLOSSARY

Abscess A localized accumulation of pus.

Action The way in which a horse moves its legs at each gait. The term covers the straightness of the movements, how high the horse lifts its feet off the ground, and the amount of flexion of the joints.

Aged Any horse older than eight years is said to be aged.

Antibiotic A drug that kills bacteria in or on the horse.

Bacteria Microscopic single-celled organisms that live in or on larger creatures such as the horse.

Bars (1) The hard stretches of gum between the last incisor tooth and the first molar tooth on which the bit rests. (2) The ends of the hoof wall, which extend from the heels towards the centre of the sole.

Bone The substance that makes up the skeleton of the horse. It is also used to refer to the circumference of the cannon bone as an indication of the horse's size and potential weight-bearing capacity.

Boxy feet Narrow, upright feet with small frogs and closed heels. Feet with this shape can cause problems, because they do not absorb concussion properly so they may put excessive strain on the legs.

Breaking out This is when a horse begins to sweat again, when it has already cooled off after exercise.

Breed A variety of horse (or other animal) consisting of a group of individuals that share the same genetic and physical characteristics and pass these to their offspring.

Bringing up Gradually bringing a horse back into work after a rest at grass, and usually into a stabled lifestyle.

Broken down A term used of a horse that has suffered a severe sprain of a flexor tendon.

Canine tooth This tooth is not always present in horses. When it is present, usually in male horses, it is called the tush and lies behind the incisor teeth.

Cartilage A substance that covers the joint surfaces of bones to form a smooth, moving surface.

Cast (in a stable or box) A horse becomes cast when it lies down or rolls in a confined space, and is unable to stand up again because it is stuck.

Cast a shoe A horse is said to have cast a shoe when a shoe comes off by accident.

Cereals Grasses that have been developed to provide seeds as food are called cereals. Examples include barley, oats, and wheat.

Clean legs (1) Legs free from blemishes or swellings, such as splints or thickened tendons. (2) Legs with little or no feather.

Clenches The end of each horseshoe nail is bent over to hold the nail in place, and the resulting hook is called a clench.

Cold-blood A heavy horse descended from the primitive Forest Horse of northern Europe.

Coloured horse A horse whose coat has large, distinct areas of white hair and black or brown hair. (Coats of more than two colours are called "odd-coloured".)

Colt A young male horse that has not been castrated.

Common-bred A horse of indeterminate breeding, usually with a low proportion of Thoroughbred blood.

Concentrates The food given to provide high levels of nutrition in a small volume.

Concussion (1) Shock or jarring that affects the feet and legs and is caused by percussion of the foot on hard surfaces. (2) Unconsciousness or temporary brain injury caused by a blow on the head.

Condition The horse's level of fitness or fatness. A horse in "soft" condition has flabby muscles and possibly extra fat; one in "hard" condition has well-toned muscles and no surplus fat.

Conformation The way a horse is put together.

Dam A horse's mother.

Diastema The technical name for the bars of the mouth.

Dishing Faulty action in which a horse throws its front feet out to each side instead of moving its legs straight.

Dominant gene A gene whose influence is greater than that of similar genes. For instance, among the genes for coat colour, grey is dominant over all others.

Draught horse A horse used for pulling heavy loads.

Dumped toe Poor foot shape caused by bad farriery. The foot is rasped so that the toe is cut off short, instead of the shoe being made to fit the foot, or the wall of the hoof being trimmed properly.

Entire A male horse that has not been castrated.

Feather Long, coarse hair on a horse's fetlocks and lower legs.

Fibre Also known as cellulose, this is the tough material that strengthens the leaves and stems of plants. Feeds with a high proportion of fibre, such as grass and hay, are called roughage.

Filly A young female horse (up to four years old) before she has had a foal.

Flehmen A behavioural response in which the horse opens its mouth and curls up its upper lip.

Folic acid A vitamin needed for blood cell formation.

Fungal spores The microscopic particles by which fungae spread through the air. They can trigger allergies in some horses.

Gait A pattern of leg movements. The gaits common to all horses are walk, trot, canter, and gallop. Special gaits particular to certain breeds include the paso, done by the Peruvian Paso, and the tölt, a speciality of the Icelandic pony.

Galls Swellings or sore, rubbed areas caused by badly fitting tack.

Galvayne's groove A groove down the upper-corner incisor teeth, used to give an approximate age for older horses.

Gelding A castrated male horse.

Going The condition of the ground, and the extent to which it affects a horse's movements. (For example, "hard going" is hard ground, and "heavy going" is deep mud that clings to the horse's feet.)

Good doer A horse that needs only a small amount of food to stay in good health and condition.

Haemoglobin The substance in red blood cells that carries oxygen and carbon dioxide.

Half-bred A horse with one parent that is Thoroughbred and one that is of a different breed.

Hand A unit of measurement for horses, which is equal to 4 in (10 cm).

Hard mouth A "hard-mouthed" horse is unresponsive to rein aids. This problem is caused by bad, heavy-handed riding, which damages the surfaces of the bars of the mouth, and deadens the nerves in the area.

Heating Describes feed that gives a horse too much energy and makes it excitable.

Heavy horse A very large, heavily built horse developed for its great strength.

Hierarchy A social grouping of horses, or other animals, in which the members have different levels of importance. The most dominant horses are at the top of the hierarchy, and the most submissive ones are at the bottom.

Hogged mane A mane that has been shorn off down to the neck.

Hot-blood A horse of Thoroughbred or Arab breeding.

Incisors The front teeth, used for biting grass and other food.

Infundibulum An indentation exposed on the biting surface of the incisor teeth at certain stages of wear.

In hand A way of leading a horse from the ground (particularly in show classes).

Instinct Automatic behaviour that the horse does not have to learn but appears to know from birth.

Keratin A protein that is the main element in hard tissue such as hoof horn.

Lactic acid Substance produced by muscle fibres during exercise. It can cause muscle damage if it is not quickly removed by the circulation.

Ligament Fibrous, cord-like structure that attaches one bone to another.

Light horse A finely built horse bred for speed rather than strength.

Light of bone A term used for a horse with an inadequate bone circumference for its build.

Lungeing A way of exercising a horse from the ground. The horse moves around a handler, who controls it with a long rein.

Mare A mature female horse.

Molars Large teeth with broad, flat top surfaces, found at the back of the mouth. They are used for grinding up food.

Nappy Used to describe a horse that will not go in the required direction, usually through wilfulness rather than fear.

Near side The horse's left side.

Off side The horse's right side.

Pace (1) The speed of the horse at a certain gait. In order of speed, the paces are: collected (slowest), working, medium, extended. (2) A specific two-beat gait where both legs on the same side move at the same time.

Parasite A living organism that lives on and off another creature. It feeds off food ingested by the host animal, or feeds from the animal itself, but gives no benefit in return.

Percussion The impact of a horse's foot as it hits the ground.

Pigment An element within the skin, horn, or hair that gives it its colour.

Pony A horse smaller than 14 hands 2 inches (1.47 m) when fully grown.

Poor doer A horse that needs a large amount of food to stay in good health or maintain condition.

Profile The shape of the horse's nose when seen from the side. It may be straight, convex (a "Roman nose"), or concave ("dished").

Pure-bred Another name for a Thoroughbred.

Pus The matter formed by accumulation of bacteria and dead white blood cells when there is a localized infection.

Recessive gene A gene whose influence is weaker than all other similar ones. Its influence is only passed on to offspring if both parents have that gene.

Roughage Long-stemmed plant material, which makes up most of a horse's diet.

Roughing off The process by which a fit horse in hard work is prepared for total rest at grass.

Scope Athletic ability, especially for jumping.

Season Also known as oestrus, this is the time during which a mare is able to conceive a foal.

Sire A horse's father.

Sound horse (1) A horse that is not lame. (2) At time of sale, a horse without any problems that will affect its usefulness.

Stale To pass urine.

Stallion An uncastrated adult male horse.

Staring coat A coat in which the hairs stick up and look dull.

Tack The equipment worn by a horse, hence the term tacking up.

Tendon A fibrous, cord-like structure that links a muscle to a bone.

True to type Means that the horse has the same physical characteristics as its parents and other typical members of its breed.

Type A group of horses that are not genetically similar and do not breed true to type, but which have a broadly similar body shape.

Vice An undesirable behavioural habit.

Virus Microscopic infectious agent. There are no practical anti-viral drugs.

Warm-blood A horse whose ancestors include both cold-bloods and hot-bloods.

White line The junction between the horn of the hoof wall and that of the sole.

Whorl A small circular pattern on the coat, with the hairs radiating outwards from the centre.

Wind A horse's breathing.

Wisping A form of skin massage in which a wisp or massage pad is brought down hard and repeatedly on a horse's muscles, to tone them and improve circulation.

Wolf tooth A small molar tooth not always present and usually removed to prevent bitting problems.

ADDITIONAL INFORMATION

Money-saving tips

The welfare of your horse should come before all other considerations, and certainly before financial matters. The following points, however, should reduce the costs of horse care.

• Consider clubbing together with other horse-owners and keeping all your horses in one place, taking turns to look after the horses and do the chores. This will give you some of the benefits of keeping a horse at livery, without the cost of livery fees.

• Set up a mutual lending arrangement for equipment that is not often used (such as clippers).

• For routine veterinary procedures (such as vaccination) and farrier's visits, get together with other owners so that the vet or farrier can visit you all on the same day. The visiting fees will be cheaper, and it will save the vet or farrier from making several trips to the same area.

• Think hard before you buy anything, to make sure that you need it. If you are not sure, seek expert advice from your vet, farrier, saddler, or riding school instructor. When you do buy new feed or equipment, buy the best quality; it will last much longer, and be much better for your horse, than cheaper brands.

• If your horse is stabled, make sure that the bed is deep enough. A thin bed is a false economy. It does not protect the horse from injuring itself on the floor, so the horse may need veterinary treatment or even be unrideable; also, it does not keep a horse warm enough, so you will pay more for feed and rugs.

Time-saving tips

Because you have voluntarily accepted the responsibility of keeping a horse, you owe it to the animal to make its life as pleasant as possible. Having said that, there are some points to bear in mind if your time is limited by work or family commitments.

• A mutual horse-care arrangement will save time as well as money. Make sure that everyone involved agrees beforehand when they can be there for the horses, and you all divide the tasks so that nobody ends up doing too much. In this way, each of the group members can ensure adequate care for their horse without having to be there all day.

• Make a list of every single task that you have to do for your horse, then arrange them in order of priority. Top of the list should be jobs that directly affect the horse: exercise, grooming, mucking out (if stabled), daily check (if living out).

• Plan ahead and allocate sufficient time for tasks that do not have to be done daily, for example thorough tack cleaning, picking up droppings from grazing land, tidying the yard and muck heap.

• For infrequent jobs such as worming, use a year planner so that you can see instantly when they have to be done. As soon as the task has been taken care of, note on your planner the next time it has to be done. Every time the vet or farrier comes, make your next routine appointment while they are still with you. Planning ahead in this way will save you from constantly worrying about these tasks, and conversely will also ensure that you do not leave it too long before attending to them.

• If you don't have time to mix your own feeds, don't be fussy about using pre-mixed feeds; these feeds are carefully formulated for different types of horse or pony at various levels of work. (Ask your vet which type or brand would be best for your horse.)

Insurance

As well as cover for your horse, you will need insurance for tack and other equipment, any stables and other buildings that you own, and yourself. Your vet, or a local riding school proprietor, is likely to know which companies process claims with few problems.

• Have your horse and equipment accurately valued.

• Read the policy carefully, preferably with expert help, so you understand exactly what it does and doesn't cover.

• Carry out all correspondence in writing and keep copies of all your letters for your reference.

• Keep your insurance policy number handy in case of sudden accidents or problems.

Alternatives to owning

If you cannot afford to buy your own horse, consider shared ownership or taking a horse on loan. Joint owners share the actual price of the horse as well as the cost of its upkeep. A horse on loan still belongs to its owner, but the person using it takes care of it and may have to pay most of the costs of keeping it.

• Joint horse-owners should work out beforehand, and put down in writing, who will do which chores at what times. They must also agree on a riding programme that gives each person a fair amount of riding time without over-tiring the horse.

• Before a horse goes out on loan, a legally binding agreement must be drawn up by a solicitor. The agreement should include how long the loan home can have the use of the horse, how the horse will be kept, what may or may not be done with it, and who is responsible for paying for vets' and farriers' visits and for insurance premiums.

• Some horse rescue charities let horses go out on loan, but these animals need expert, caring homes because they may have physical or psychological problems.

• Any owner loaning a horse will probably want to see how you intend to keep it, and how well you are able to ride and handle it.

USEFUL ADDRESSES

Royal Society for the Prevention of Cruelty to Animals
RSPCA Headquarters, The Causeway, Horsham, West Sussex   RH12 1HG
Tel. 01403 264181

Scottish Society for the Prevention of Cruelty to Animals
19 Melville Street, Edinburgh, Scotland   EH3 7PL
Tel. 0131 6635507

Ulster Society for the Prevention of Cruelty to Animals
11 Drumview Road, Ballymagarrick, Lisburn, Northern Ireland   BT27 6YF
Tel. 01232 813126

Irish Society for the Prevention of Cruelty to Animals
Rathmines Road, Dublin, Republic of Ireland
Tel. 010 3531 4977222

Other charities for equines

Blue Cross Horse Protection Scheme
Blue Cross Field Centre, Shilton Road, Burford, Oxfordshire   OX8 4PF
Tel. 01993 822651
Takes in and rescues horses, which may be loaned to suitable homes.

The Home of Rest for Horses
Dept. Y1, Westcroft Stables, Speen Farm, Slad Lane, Lacey Green, Bucks.   HP27 0PP
Tel. 01494 448464
Provides retirement care for horses, and is also the largest supporter of veterinary research for horse welfare.

The International League for the Protection of Horses
Anne Colvin House, Snetterton, Norfolk
Tel. 01953 498682
Concerned with the welfare of horses internationally, the League has worked hard to ban the transport of live horses for slaughter abroad.

The Donkey Sanctuary
Sidmouth, Devon   EX10 0NU
Tel. 01395 578222; Fax 01395 579266
Rescues donkeys, and provides help and information on donkey welfare.

The Donkey Breed Society
The Hermitage, Pootings, Edenbridge, Kent   TN8 6SD
Tel. 01732 864414
Provides advice and information on donkey welfare and breeding.

Advice on horse care

The British Horse Society
The British Equestrian Centre, Stoneleigh Park, Kenilworth, Warwickshire   CV8 2LR
Tel. 01203 696697; Fax 01203 692351
Among its other functions, the Society provides advice on horse care.

British Veterinary Association
7 Mansfield Street, London W1M 0AT
Tel. 0171 636 6541

British Equine Veterinary Association
Hartham Park, Corsham, Wiltshire SN13 0QB
Tel. 01249 715723

Riding for the Disabled Association
Avenue R, National Agricultural Centre, Stoneleigh Park, Kenilworth, Warwickshire CV8 2LR
Tel. 01203 696510
The RDA has volunteer groups who can give help and advice.

Technical advice

The Farriers' Registration Council
P.O. Box 49, East of England Showground, Peterborough, Cambridgeshire   PE2 6GU
Tel. 01733 371171; Fax 01733 371103
Licenses all farriers in the UK.

Farmkey
England House, Beaumont Road, Banbury, Oxon.   OX16 7RH
Tel. 01295 252544; Fax 01295 251049
National freeze-branding service.

Equibrand
Church Street, Charwelton, Northants. NN11 3YT
Tel. 01327 262444; Fax 01327 260771
Hoof branding for horses.

Animalcare Ltd.
Common Road, Dunnington, York YO1 5RU
Tel. 01904 488661
Produce Identichip, a microchip for horse security. Horses fitted with microchips are registered with HorseSafe (see below).

HorseSafe
P.O. Box 48, St. Neots, Huntingdon, Cambs.   PE19 4JY
Tel. 01480 403230; Fax 01480 403604
National computerized anti-theft register for horses.

INDEX

ACKNOWLEDGMENTS

Author's acknowledgments
The author would like to thank
the staff of Gillham House
Veterinary Group for their
help and patience during
the preparation of this book.

Publisher's acknowledgments
Dorling Kindersley would like
to thank the following people:

Nereide and John Goodman for
use of the horses, helpers, and
facilities at Wellington Riding Ltd.

Ascot Stables Ltd for use of the
show stable at Old House Farm.

Owners and horses at Wellington
Riding Ltd: Heather Berryman
(Rose); Jackie Caldwell (Tikka's
Dream); Peter Caldwell
(Pendragon); Philippa Earthy
(Fergus); Sarah Elmslie (Five &
Twenty); Nereide Goodman
(Wellington Laska and Wellington
Trafalgar); Tessa Lawton (Nivelle);
Richard Morrish (Milarochy Bay);
Fiona Pavitt (Boothlands Azzaro);
Robert Pickles (Wellington
Asyllus); Kathleen Ramey
(Catherston Dear Edward); Anna
Shelton (Kerry); Theresa Hulton
(Captain Morgan); Pat Watts
(Brandysnap).

At Ascot Stables Ltd:
Sheila Baigent (Puzzle).

All the staff at Wellington Riding
Ltd for their help and patience
especially Beverley Davies, Alex
Ehrmann, and Suzanne Judd.

Ralph Butler, Beverley Davies,
Harriet Green, Samuel Harpur,
Katie John, Suzanne Judd, Shelly
Moores, David Sheerin, Claudia
Steele, Colin Vogel for modelling.

Emma Butcher, Anna Shelton,
and Amanda Webb for assistance.

Clive Duffin for farriery.

Mark Runiewicz for the use
of his trailer.

Hilary Bird for the index.

Becky Halls for picture research.
Rachel Leach for additional
picture research.

Dorling Kindersley would also
like to thank Cam Equestrian Ltd
and Ride Away for the loan
of saddlery, clothing, and
equipment; Clayton Equine Safety
for the Equipack first-aid pack;
B and J Dance and Dengie Crops
Ltd for horse feeds; Fieldguard
for rubber matting; Hemcore for
hemp bedding.

KEY: t top, b bottom, c centre,
l left, r right,

Illustrations
All illustrations by Andrew Macdonald except for
Joanna Cameron 26c, 27cl,tr; Tony Graham 24,
26bl,cr; Janos Marffy 46; Sean Milne 10; Dan
Wright 27cr.

Photography
Additional photography by Peter Anderson,
Peter Chadwick, Geoff Dann, Mike Dunning,
Andreas Einsiedel, Neil Fletcher, John Glover,
Steve Gorton, Anna Hodgson, Colin Keates,
Dave King, Bob Langrish, Andrew McRobb, Ray
Moller, Gary Ombler, Roger Philips, Tim Ridley,
Matthew Ward.
Biofotos/Heather Angel 84c; Bruce Coleman
Ltd/Jeff Foott Productions 40b/Flip de Nooyer
85tr/William S. Paton 10cr/Dr Eckart Pott 10b,
82br/Hans Reinhard 64t/Gunter Ziesler 40c;
courtesy Equibrand 114bl,c, 180cr; Robert
Harding Picture Library 84t; Michael Holford 8–9;
Kit Houghton 30cr, 35cl, 79tl, 80t,br, 82t, 98t;
The Image Bank/Jack Ward 36t; Derek
Knottenbelt/University of Liverpool 122b,
123tl,bl, 124clb, bl, 125t,c, 126cl, 127bl, 128cl,bl,
129t,c, 130t,c,b, 131t,bl,bc, 132br, 133t,c, 137,
138c,b, 139b; Bob Langrish 22bl, 69bl, 79tr,
181b, 92–3, 95t, 183tl; Microscopix Photo
Library/Andrew Syred 21tr; Only Horses Picture
Agency 78b, 113br; Harry Smith Horticultural
Collection 82cr,bl,bc, 83cr, 84br, 85c,cl; Tony
Stone Images 78t, 99cr; ZEFA 36b, 77tr.

p. 11 **Highland pony** – *Monarch of Dykes*
     Countess of Swinton

pp. 12–13 **Hack** –
Mr and Mrs D Curtis
Riding pony, cob, hunter –
Robert Oliver

p. 14 **Dorsal strip**e – *Fruich of Dykes*
Countess of Swinton
Dun – *Montemere O'Nora*
Nan Thurman

p. 15 **Blaze** – *Spooks*
Peter Munt
Snip – *Hippolyte*
Haras Nationale de Pau

p. 18 **Arab** – *Muskhari Silver*
Janet and Anne Connolly, Silver Fox Arabians,
West Midlands
Ardennais – *Trojan*
Charlie Pinney, Egrement Farm, Payhembury,
Honiton, Devon

p. 46 t – *Noaner*
Instituto Incremento Ippico di Crema

The publishers would like to make it clear
that no horses were injured during photography
for this book.